# Planning, Funding, and Implementing a Child Abuse Prevention Project

Rebekah L. Dorman

Douglas J. Moore

Caroline A. Schaerfl

CWLA Press ★ Washington, DC

CWLA Press is an imprint of the Child Welfare League of America. The Child Welfare League of America (CWLA), the nation's oldest and largest membership-based child welfare organization, is committed to engaging all Americans in promoting the well-being of children and protecting every child from harm.

CHILD WELFARE LEAGUE OF AMERICA, INC.
440 First Street, NW, Third Floor, Washington, DC 20001-2085
E-mail: books@cwla.org

CURRENT PRINTING (last digit)
10 9 8 7 6 5 4 3 2 1

Cover design by Luke Johnson

Photo credits: front cover, lower left, Claire Flanders; front cover, upper right, Jeffrey High; back cover, Jeffrey High

Printed in the United States of America

ISBN # 0-87868-562-6

*Library of Congress Cataloging-in-Publication Data*
Planning, funding, and implementing a child abuse prevention project /
    Rebekah L. Dorman . . . [et al.].
        p.        cm.
    Includes bibliographical references.
    ISBN 0-87868-562-6
    1. Child abuse—United States—Prevention—Handbooks, manuals,
etc. 2. Child welfare—United States—Handbooks, manuals, etc.
I. Dorman, Rebekah L.
HV741.P498  1998                                                98-24861
362.76'7'0973—dc21                                                CIP

# *For the Children*

An old man was walking along the ocean shore early one morning. He looked down the beach and saw a human figure moving like a dancer. He began to walk faster to catch up. Coming close, he saw a young woman reach down into the sand, pick something up, and gently throw it into the ocean.

As he got closer, he called out, "Good morning! What are you doing?"

The young woman paused, looked up, and replied, "Throwing starfish into the ocean."

"Why are you throwing starfish back into the ocean?"

"Because the sun is up, and the tide is going out. And if I don't throw them in, they'll die."

"But young woman, don't you realize that there are miles and miles of beach with starfish all along them? You can't possibly make a difference!"

The young woman listened politely, then bent down, picked up another starfish, and gently threw it into the sea, past the breaking waves. She turned to the old man and said quietly, "I made a difference to that one."

*—Anonymous*

# Contents

## List of Tables

## Case Studies

# Acknowledgments

We would first like to express our gratitude to Dr. Lisa Pion-Berlin, former Executive Director of Ohio Children's Trust Fund, for the original concept of Statewide Teamwork for Abuse Resources (STAR), as well as for her confidence in us regarding implementation of the project.

We are indebted to the Ohio Children's Trust Fund Board for their financial support of this innovative project.

We also extend our appreciation and thanks to the many child abuse prevention professionals who participated in the STAR forums and to the many professionals across Ohio who participated in the field-testing of the manual through surveys and/or focus groups. They provided us with an invaluable "reality check" on the applicability of the manual for their prevention work.

Finally, we express appreciation to Sharon Spottsville for her assistance with the chapter on cultural competence and to Erzsi Somogyi and Diane James for assistance in the preparation of the final manuscript.

*Rebekah L. Dorman, Ph.D.*
Vice President
Applewood Centers, Inc.
Cleveland, Ohio

# Introduction

Preventing child abuse is an endeavor that requires equal parts caring, optimism, and pragmatism. We must care deeply about children, be optimistic about human beings' capabilities for change, and be pragmatic about how to work with families to bring about positive change.

This book assumes that caring and optimism already reside with the reader. It therefore concentrates on the pragmatic—how to translate the abstract notion of prevention into a blueprint for action. In an era when prevention has increasingly gained recognition as the most prudent and cost-effective strategy for addressing child abuse and neglect, it is surprising that so little has been written about how to actually do it. The literature is replete with justifications for prevention and accounts of individual child abuse prevention projects, but there has been little written about general strategies and procedures, or the "nitty-gritty" details of developing and implementing a successful child abuse prevention project.

This manual was designed to fill that void. It grew out of the experiences of more than 100 child abuse prevention projects across the state of Ohio. Our goal was to integrate the abstract principles of program development and prevention with the real world experiences and challenges faced by prevention projects on a daily basis. Above all, we have attempted to describe prevention as a process occurring in the real world.

In fact, the development of this manual was itself a child abuse prevention project funded by the Ohio Children's Trust Fund in 1990.

The idea for the manual grew out of conversations between Dr. Lisa Pion-Berlin, the Director of Ohio Children's Trust Fund at that time; Dr. Douglas Moore, the Director of Research at the Child Guidance Center of Greater Cleveland at that time; and myself.

In the course of reviewing hundreds of grant applications, Dr. Pion-Berlin had observed that many of the professionals attempting child abuse prevention work came from such related disciplines as education, child welfare, and family services, and though they were well trained in their own field, they often had little specific expertise in child abuse prevention. On the other hand, we also knew that many prevention projects throughout Ohio were engaged in innovative and meaningful prevention efforts.

Thus the idea for Statewide Teamwork for Abuse Resources (STAR) was born with a grant to the Research and Training Department of the Child Guidance Center. The goal of STAR was to review current resources on such disparate topics as management techniques, funding sources, cultural issues, and personnel administration, in addition to child abuse prevention, and then distill the information that would be of practical use to someone attempting a child abuse prevention project.

To obtain real-life examples of the procedures detailed in the manual, we tapped into the experiences of 20 prevention projects around the state that had received funding from the Trust Fund. Three forums were held during that first year in which grantees generously shared their experiences and opinions—and we listened. That experience made us even more convinced of the need for this manual. Although we were continually impressed by the breadth and depth of the work being done in Ohio, we also observed how isolated the staff of each project felt and how much they wanted to have access to others' ideas and advice. Grantees identified numerous topics for inclusion in the manual and shared their projects' successes and failures. All of that material was then integrated into the first draft of the manual.

With the first draft of the manual in hand, we then applied to the Trust Fund for a second year of funding so that the manual could be field tested. Prevention projects that received funding from the Ohio Children's Trust Fund were offered the opportunity to use and evaluate the manual either through a survey, a focus group, or both. More than 80 projects volunteered and kindly shared with us their suggestions for improving the manual.

The unique journey of STAR has produced, we hope, a resource that will help professional and layperson alike, in their quest to help children and families. Without the pragmatic means to implement successful prevention programs, our caring and our optimism will have no impact.

# Child Abuse and Its Prevention: An Overview

In Cleveland, Ohio, a home visitor is explaining potty training to a teenage mother; in Wichita, Kansas, a classroom teacher is telling children about the private parts of their bodies; in San Antonio, Texas, a public service announcement on television asserts, "Don't shake the baby!" These are the many faces of child abuse prevention in America today.

Over the past three decades, our awareness of the grim problem of child abuse has grown, and so have our efforts to prevent it. Federal legislation mandates research, information dissemination, and demonstration programs; Children's Trust Funds lead prevention efforts in many states; and numerous community-based programs have started up across the country. Child abuse has become part of our national consciousness.

Yet, despite our awareness and these accomplishments, we don't have "tried and true" prevention models. The complexity of the problem, the limited resources society provides to address it, and the lack of well-designed evaluations assessing the impact of programs on families have all contributed to that situation. But there is no doubt that prevention is the best hope for substantially reducing the problem and improving the lives of millions of children and their parents.

## Impact on Child Victims

A commitment to child abuse prevention often grows out of a deep concern for the children and the impact of maltreatment upon their bodies and minds.

1

The range and type of physical injuries resulting from maltreatment are indeed disturbing but are only the most obvious sign of the damage that has been done [Feldman 1997; Reichert 1997]. Numerous studies have documented the types of effects children suffer in all realms of development. Many emotional, social, behavioral, and cognitive deficits linger long after the physical wounds have healed.

The pain of the victims and the impact upon child development is well-documented [Aber et al. 1989]. Sometimes the children suffer quietly, other times their painful experiences translate into aggressive behavior or even the sexual molestation of other children. And so the next generation of perpetrators is created out of this generation of victims. Treatment can help, but it is far better to prevent the pain, then to try to help children cope with it. The impact upon the child will vary depending upon characteristics of the abuse and of the child. The impact will be more severe if the abuse begins when the child is young, continues for a long period of time, and is done by someone closely connected to the child, such as the parent. From a developmental perspective, a child's reaction to abuse changes from initial symptoms of fear and confusion to more permanent changes in attitudes and behavior. The earlier and more long-lasting the abuse, the more its effects will be integrated into the child's personality [Kempe 1997]. For prevention professionals, then, it is clear that if we are unable to intervene before abuse has occurred, there is still an urgency to intervene and prevent further abuse as early in the maltreating relationship as possible.

Although children will react individually to the maltreatment they suffer, research has now accumulated that describes widely observed effects among the victims. These effects include poor ability to relate to peers or adults, developmental delays, cognitive deficits and academic difficulties, aggressiveness, and low self-esteem (often accompanied by depression) [English 1998; Kempe 1997; Aber & Cichetti 1984].

Children who experienced neglect only, have, as a group, been studied much less than physically abused children. However, studies indicate that they also demonstrate poor social ability, heightened aggressiveness, delays in intellectual and linguistic abilities, academic difficulties, and poor coping ability [see Crouch & Milner 1993 for a review]. Although more research on neglected children is needed, there is no doubt that the omission of appropriate caregiving can be as devastating for the child as the infliction of physical harm.

The victims of sexual abuse whose maltreatment experience is of a different nature than those who suffered physical abuse or neglect display effects both similar and different than other maltreatment victims. Low self-esteem, anxiety, depression, impaired sense of self, interpersonal difficulties, anger, and aggression are problems most commonly noted during childhood [Briere & Elliott 1994]. But, again, there is no well-defined single pattern of symptoms or problems resulting from sexual abuse [Beutler et al. 1994].

The short- and long-term consequences of child maltreatment affect communities too. Immediate financial costs include investigation of reports, treatment of victims and offenders, placement of children into foster care, and prosecution of offenders. Investigations of long-term effects find a relationship between childhood maltreatment and criminality. A 1992 study sponsored by the National Institutes of Justice [Widom 1992] found that maltreatment increases the victim's likelihood of arrest as a juvenile by 53%, as an adult by 38%, and for a violent crime by 38%. For females, being a victim of abuse or neglect increases the likelihood of arrest by 77%.

The impact of the abuse may also be felt by the next generation. Though most abused children do not grow up to be abusers, research indicates that parents who were abused as children maltreat their own children at six times the rate of the general population [Kaufman & Zigler 1987]. Though the cycle of abuse is not inevitable, it is a real consequence in about one-third of the families in which the child victim is now a parent. The human cost of this family legacy is, of course, incalculable.

# Definitions of Child Abuse and Neglect

The Child Abuse Prevention and Treatment Act (CAPTA) is the federal legislation that defines maltreatment. First authorized in 1974, CAPTA was amended and reauthorized in October 1996 and defines child abuse and neglect, at a minimum, as any recent act or failure to act

> *Resulting in* imminent risk of serious harm, death, serious physical or emotional harm, sexual abuse, or exploitation
>
> *Of a child* (person under the age of 18, unless the child protection law of the State in which the child resides specifies a younger age for cases not involving sexual abuse)
>
> *By a parent or caretaker* (including any employee of a residential facility or any staff person providing out-of-home care) who is responsible for the child's welfare. [DHHS 1996b]

CAPTA's definition of sexual abuse follows:

> Employment, use, persuasion, inducement, enticement, or coercion of any child to engage in, or assist any other person to engage in, any sexually explicit conduct or any simulation of such conduct for the purpose of producing any visual depiction of such conduct; or rape, and in cases of caretaker or interfamilial relationships, statutory rape, molestation, prostitution, or other form of sexual exploitation of children, or incest with children. [DHHS 1996b]

This federal act provides a minimum standard for behaviors that can be considered maltreatment, but each state is responsible for providing definitions of abuse and neglect within the civil and criminal context. These civil laws, or statutes, vary by state and describe the circumstances and conditions that obligate mandated reporters to report known or suspected cases of abuse. Though the state statute provides definitions, in reality, "to a considerable extent, state legislatures have left it up to professionals in the field to interpret what constitutes 'abuse' or 'neglect'" [Sedlak & Broadhurst 1996, p. 2-7].

The lack of clear and consistent definitions directing program goals is a problem often cited in reviews of child abuse prevention programs [Fink & McCloskey 1990]. And, indeed, there is no national consensus. Agreement can usually be reached regarding the most extreme cases, but it is those less extreme circumstances where consensus is most difficult. For example, since no statute outlaws all physical punishment of children, when does a spanking "cross the line" and become abusive? At what age can a child be left alone at home without this being considered neglectful? Child protective workers make maltreatment determinations on a daily basis as they receive and investigate reports. For child abuse prevention professionals, specific definitions are important because they inform project goals and services. You must be clear on what you are trying to prevent, before you try to prevent it.

CONTACT INFORMATION: You can obtain state laws from your local child protection agency or from the National Clearinghouse on Child Abuse and Neglect Information. The Clearinghouse maintains a State Statutes Desk that summarizes state laws in nontechnical language to make them useful to nonlegal professionals. You may access laws via their website: *http://www. calib.com/nccanch*, or you may contact them at 1-800-FYI-3366 or by e-mail at nccanch@calib.com.

## The Four Types of Maltreatment

Legal definitions do not provide adequate descriptions of the types of maltreatment that occur. Below are descriptions provided by the National Clearinghouse on Child Abuse and Neglect Information. (The Clearinghouse was established by CAPTA and is mandated to gather and disseminate information related to child abuse and neglect.)

### Physical Abuse
The infliction of physical injury as a result of punching, beating, kicking, biting, burning, shaking, or otherwise harming a child. The par-

ent or caretaker may not have intended to hurt the child; rather, the injury may have resulted from overly harsh discipline or physical punishment.

### Child Neglect

The failure to provide for the child's basic needs. Neglect can be physical, educational, or emotional. Physical neglect includes refusal of or delay in seeking health care, abandonment, expulsion from the home or refusal to allow a runaway to return home, and inadequate supervision. Educational neglect includes the allowance of chronic truancy, failure to enroll a child of mandatory school age in school, and failure to attend to a special educational need. Emotional neglect includes such actions as marked inattention to the child's needs for affection, refusal of or failure to provide needed psychological care, spouse abuse in the child's presence, and permission for drug or alcohol use by the child.

### Sexual Abuse

Fondling a child's genitals, intercourse, incest, rape, sodomy, exhibitionism, and commercial exploitation through prostitution or the production of pornographic materials.

### Emotional Abuse

Acts or omissions by the parent or other caregivers that have caused, or could cause, serious behavioral, cognitive, emotional, or mental disorders. The parents/caregivers may use extreme or bizarre forms of punishment, such as confinement of a child in a dark closet. Less severe acts include habitual scapegoating, belittling, or rejecting treatment. Emotional abuse is almost always present when other forms of maltreatment are identified.

## The Incidence of Maltreatment

Given that there are no nationally agreed-upon definitions of maltreatment, how are we able to arrive at an annual incidence rate? The most straightforward and conservative approach is to use official statistics gathered from child protective service (CPS) agencies.[1] These numbers refer to cases substantiated by a state child protective agency using the guidelines of state law.

Investigations by CPS across the nation determined that more than 1 million children were victims of substantiated or indicated child abuse and neglect in 1995.[2] This statistic translates into a rate of 15 children per 1,000 who were victims during 1995. This is, however, most certainly an underestimate of the actual number of child victims. There is widespread agreement that many cases of maltreatment never come to the attention of authorities, and that some real reported cases lack enough evidence for the worker to make a finding of either substantiated or indicated.

How much of an underestimate is it? The Third National Incidence Study of Child Abuse and Neglect (NIS-3) [Sedlak & Broadhurst 1996] attempts to answer that question. Commissioned by the federal government and conducted in 1993, the study does not rely on official statistics. Instead, the researchers surveyed 5,600 community professionals to identify maltreated children who may or may not be known to authorities. Based upon those data, the researchers estimated the much higher incidence of 1.5 million children, or 42 per 1,000, who actually experienced harm as a result of maltreatment.

Furthermore, by comparing the results of this last incidence study to the prior study conducted in 1986, they conclude that there has been a sizeable increase in actual incidence. For example, the number of *seriously* injured children quadrupled in that time period from approximately 143,000 to nearly 570,000. One of the most disturbing

---

[1] Unless otherwise indicated, statistics are derived from *Child Maltreatment 1995: Reports from the States to the National Child Abuse and Neglect Data System*.

[2] *Substantiated* means that an allegation of maltreatment was confirmed according to the level of evidence required by state law or state policy. *Indicated* is a term used in some states when there is insufficient evidence to substantiate a case under state law or policy, but there is reason to suspect that maltreatment occurred or that there is risk of future maltreatment.

conclusions of the NIS-3 is the fact that, despite this increased incidence rate, the number of cases investigated by child protective
authorities has remained constant. These numbers tell us that a de-
creasing percentage of actual cases are being handled by the authorities. The authors suggest that the CPS system has simply reached its
capacity to respond to reports [Sedlack & Broadhurst 1996].

Neglect continues to be the most frequently reported and substantiated type of maltreatment. Based upon actual CPS cases, more than
half (52%) of all victims suffered neglect, 25% physical abuse, 13%
sexual abuse, 5% emotional maltreatment, 3% medical neglect, and
14% other types of maltreatment. Most children suffer more than one
type of maltreatment, since emotional abuse is almost always present
when another type of maltreatment occurs. Girls experience maltreatment more often than boys, because of their higher risk to be sexually
abused. (Overall, 52% of victims were female and 47% were male.)
According to NIS-3, girls experience sexual abuse at more than three
times the rate of boys.

More than half of the child victims were younger than age 7 and
fatalities were disproportionately higher among the youngest age group.
Fully 81% of the approximately 1,000 documented fatalities from maltreatment in 1995 were under 4 years of age. These numbers tells us
that, despite the many prevention programs that have come into existence, there is still much to be done.

## Who Abuses and Neglects Children?

Children face the greatest risk of being maltreated at the hands of a
biological parent. According to the NIS-3, 78% of the children reported as maltreated were abused or neglected by their birth parents.
Since most children are cared for by at least one biological parent, this
is not a surprising finding.

The dynamics of child sexual abuse are quite different. While physical abuse and neglect is the most extreme form of dysfunction in the

caregiving relationship, sexual abuse can occur outside of the caregiver-child relationship. Nearly one-half of the children were sexually abused by someone other than a parent or parent substitute, though not necessarily by a "stranger." Biological parents account for 29% of the sexual perpetrators and 25% of the children were sexually abused by a parent substitute.

## Causes of Maltreatment

The first attempts to understand the "why" of child abuse relied on single factor models with either a psychiatric or sociological emphasis (i.e., the parent was mentally ill or American society condoned the use of violence against children). That narrow focus has given way to a much more complex, dynamic view of the causes of child maltreatment. Over the past decade an ecological perspective that recognizes the complicated interplay between characteristics of the parent, child, and environment over time has emerged as the most complete theoretical model for understanding this destructive and dysfunctional behavior [Belsky & Vondra 1989]. In this view, the personal resources and history of the parent, characteristics of the child, family setting, social network and neighborhood, economic and employment factors, as well as American society at large, are all determinants of the quality of care a parent provides to her or his child.

Though our theoretical perspective may have enlarged considerably, our research base remains limited. We have, for example, little understanding of how these various personal and environmental characteristics interact to result in maltreatment or in a positive and nurturing parent-child relationship. Certain "protective" factors may counteract risk factors and ameliorate the chance of dysfunction.

More research on these protective factors may help professionals gain a better understanding of how and why such risk conditions as poverty or family stress can present developmentally threatening patterns of child rearing in some instances, while in others, families are able to buffer these conditions and provide growth-promoting developmental environments for their infants and young children [Ricciuti & Dorman 1983].

But considering the stakes, we are placed in the position of needing to take action before research provides us with a complete understanding of the dynamics of maltreatment. Even though family support programs could be beneficial for all families, limited resources mean that we must attempt to identify those most in need of help. Those factors correlated with an increased incidence of maltreatment are considered risk factors and are used by program planners to identify families most in need of intervention. In reality, these risk factors are often interrelated and one risk factor can lead to the occurrence of another [Ricciuti & Dorman 1983]. For example, a poor, young, single mother who does not obtain prenatal care and then gives birth to a child with medical problems faces the challenge of raising a child who is more difficult to care for with limited resources and support. Described below are major risk factors generally used by prevention programs seeking to serve a high-risk population.

## Poverty

Although abuse occurs across all income levels, studies consistently find that it is much more prevalent among families with low incomes. NIS-3 found that children in families with incomes below $15,000 were 25 times more likely than children in families with annual incomes above $30,000 to have been harmed or endangered by child abuse and neglect. Despite such consistent statistical evidence to the contrary, there has been a persistent myth that child abuse is "classless" and that prejudice against and greater scrutiny of poor families create this disparity.

Although most poor parents do not abuse their children, it should not surprise us that the conditions associated with poverty take a toll upon many parents and their ability to care for their children. Sedlak and Broadhurst [1996] name a number of factors associated with poverty that could account for this higher rate among poor families: transience in residence, poorer education, higher rates of substance abuse and emotional disorders, and less adequate social support systems.

No relationship between race and maltreatment incidence was found in the NIS-3. It is striking to note that this occurred despite the fact that children of color are disproportionately represented among lower income families.

## Other Risk Factors

Although our understanding of the dynamics of maltreatment has progressed far beyond simply labeling the abuser as sick, there are a number of caregiver characteristics that can play a role in its etiology. Low self-esteem, aggressiveness, poor impulse control, anxiety, and depression often characterize abusive parents [National Research Council 1993]. In addition, the parent who has unrealistic expectations of the child and developmental norms, as well as a negative attitude toward parenting, also appears to be at increased risk [English 1998]. And, as cited above, having been abused yourself makes it much more likely that you will become a perpetrator [Crouch & Milner 1993].

Over the past 20 years, substance abuse by the parent or caregiver has increasingly been cited as the reason for maltreatment. It is estimated that 50 to 80% of families involved with child protective services are dealing with a substance abuse problem [English 1998]. Domestic violence is recognized as a risk factor, both because male batterers are often child abusers as well, and because battered women are more likely to abuse their children [McKay 1994; Giles-Sims 1985].

## What Are the Indicators of Maltreatment?

Years of clinical experience with maltreated children have led to the development of many lists denoting "indicators" of maltreatment and Appendix A, Abuse Indicators, provides one such list. It is worthwhile to note that such opposite behaviors as extreme aggressiveness and extreme withdrawal both appear on the list. While certain patterns of behaviors do exist, children react in an individual fashion to trauma, and this reaction can vary widely from child to child. In addition, it is important to note that these indicators may also indicate a problem of another nature. Whether they signal maltreatment or something else, they usually reveal that a child is in need of help.

# Prevention Models

Prevention is classified into three broad categories: primary, secondary, and tertiary.

## *Primary Prevention*

Primary prevention attempts to affect individuals in a way that prevents abuse from ever occurring. It is directed at the general population and may take several different forms:

★ Public service announcements on radio and television encouraging parents to use nonviolent forms of care with children. "Take time out—don't take it out on your kids!" and "Don't shake the baby!" were the slogans of two national primary prevention campaigns implemented in the past decade.

★ Parent education programs that teach nurturing, nonviolent caregiving techniques, and appropriate expectations for children.

★ Primary prevention aimed at children and teenagers generally are school-based and focus on teaching what maltreatment is and how children can protect themselves. Sexual abuse prevention has usually been the focus of these programs. There are also programs teaching life skills and conflict resolution to prepare students for responsible adulthood.

## *Secondary Prevention*

Secondary prevention focuses on children and families considered high-risk for being a victim or perpetrator of maltreatment. Given the limited resources that exist for child abuse prevention, policymakers and funders often wish to target those considered most vulnerable. Secondary prevention programs must identify the risk factors within the population that is targeted and then direct their efforts at ameliorating the conditions associated with those risk factors.

Difficulties in implementing secondary prevention arise from the fact that a high-risk population is being targeted. Providers must be careful to advertise the program in a positive way and to recruit prospective participants so that they don't feel stigmatized by their participation. In addition, if the program is voluntary, there is the possibility that the highest risk parents are precisely those who refuse to participate or drop out. In fact, their refusal of services may be interpreted as an additional risk factor.

Examples of secondary prevention include home visiting programs for teenage mothers, respite care for families in crisis, and family resource centers in low-income neighborhoods.

### Tertiary Prevention

Tertiary prevention is aimed at perpetrators who have already maltreated and attempts to intervene to prevent further occurrences of abuse or neglect. These programs are often not voluntary, and participants are required to participate or face clear consequences, such as the removal of their children from the home. Generally, these programs are staffed by mental health professionals who work with the perpetrators to change attitudes and behavior. Examples of tertiary prevention include mental health counseling to change abusive child rearing, sex offender programs, intensive in-home services, and Parents Anonymous groups.

## What Is "State of the Art" Prevention?

If we are to embrace the ecological model of the cause of maltreatment, then the implications for prevention programs are clear and profound. As Olds and Henderson state, "The most promising approaches to prevention are those programs that are multifaceted and capable of simultaneously addressing the numerous factors that create contexts for maltreatment" [Olds & Henderson 1989, p. 725]. They argue that addressing only one dimension of a multidimensional phenomenon is unlikely to succeed. And, indeed, there are few well-documented success stories.

Some prevention programs have documented success using improved scores on paper-and-pencil measures of parenting behavior, or using parent testimonials stating that the program helped them to reduce the yelling and the hitting. But at this point only one program, the Prenatal Early Infancy Project in Elmira, Ohio, has clearly documented success in preventing the occurrence of substantiated cases of abuse and neglect over a substantial period of time (15 years) [Olds et al. 1997]. Replications are now underway to determine whether this model, originally successful with a low-income white rural population, will work equally well with urban African American families. So far, the results seem promising [Kitzman et al. 1997].

Informed by ecological theory [Bronfenbrenner 1981], the Prenatal Early Infancy Project [Olds et al. 1997] was designed as a multidimensional intervention. Using a nurse home-visiting model, the program targeted first-time pregnant women and viewed the parent-child relationship as embedded within a multilayered environment consisting of informal and formal supports and affected by the larger social and economic macrosystem [Olds 1983]. By enhancing social skills, the nurses attempted to alter parents' relationships with informal social networks and community services as well as participation in education and work.

Based in part on the successes of the Prenatal Early Infancy Project, home visiting as a mode of service delivery to families has gained in popularity in recent years. In 1991, the U.S. Advisory Board on Child Abuse and Neglect recommended universal implementation of home visitation programs to reduce the incidence of maltreatment. However, at this point no other home-visiting program has clearly demonstrated effectiveness in preventing child abuse [Barnes et al. 1995]. There are many other home-visiting initiatives now underway. Hawaii Healthy

Start and Healthy Families America are probably the highest profile of these programs, and their evaluation results are anxiously awaited.

Although other programs have not been able to document their success as rigorously or as successfully as the Prenatal Early Infancy Project, we may still find their experiences instructive. The National Center on Child Abuse and Neglect recently compiled a report on the nine community-based child abuse prevention projects that received federal funding from 1989 through 1994. This review, *Lessons Learned: The Experience of Nine Child Abuse and Neglect Prevention Programs* summarizes "best practices" guidelines based upon the experience of those programs. These guidelines are briefly described below:

★ **Be *of* the community, not just *in* the community**. Programs cannot come from the outside in; they must be part of the community fabric and run by a community-based agency with strong collaborative relationships with other agencies. A community advisory council with real decisionmaking power and accountability, as well as hiring staff indigenous to the targeted community, were two key elements.

★ **Emphasize the positive**. Beginning with the program's name, project a positive image, use community resources to support the project—including respected community leaders, strong neighborhood networks, and creative grassroots organizations. In addition, provide opportunities for recreational activities for entire families to provide some fun and strengthen staff-family relationships.

★ **Think big and start small**. Start small (e.g., in one neighborhood), so that goals are manageable and staff do not become overwhelmed. Tinker with the program to improve it, before you attempt to enlarge the program. Building a program that fits the needs and resources of the community resulted in six of the nine programs being supported financially by the community once the federal dollars ended.

★ **Design, implement, and use a strong evaluation.** Of the nine projects, none produced an evaluation that could persuasively demonstrate that their program was indeed effective. The obstacles they encountered included the following:

- Not enough money budgeted to do the evaluation

- Staff were not skilled in implementing the different phases of the evaluation

- It was difficult to locate appropriate and methodologically sound instruments to measure what they were attempting to achieve

- Measuring outcomes before the program had become stable [CSR, Inc. 1997]

CONTACT INFORMATION: The entire report of the National Center on Child Abuse and Neglect, cited above, is available on-line at *http://www.calib.com/nccanch*.

## A Critical Time

Within the past 10 years, there has been a significant shift away from focusing on deficits and toward building upon strengths in individuals, families, and communities. When families with problems are viewed as also possessing strengths, the focus of programming includes building upon those strengths, not just "fixing" the deficits. Empowerment is the word most often used in this context.

With welfare reform now a reality, it has become even more urgent for service providers to help families build their coping skills and take responsibility for themselves and their children. We are at a critical time and no one yet knows what the impact of welfare reform will be on children or families' ability to care for them. So many prevention programs have been aimed at families on welfare, and it seems clear that new programs focused on helping families make this transition are urgently needed. Although the wisdom gleaned from programs of the past still seems relevant, past experience also tells us that we won't really know until we try.

CONTACT INFORMATION: The National Child Abuse and Neglect Information Clearinghouse maintains the Child Abuse Prevention Program Database, which contains profiles of more than 300 community-based prevention programs throughout the country. The Document Database contains more than 25,000 abstracts on program development and administration, as well as evaluation. You can access both at http://www.calib.com/nccanch, or call the Clearinghouse Prevention Services desk at 1-800-FYI-3366.

## A Vision for the Future

Investing in prevention will reap benefits for all of us. It is the sensible and responsible way to confront child maltreatment. As program planners and providers, we have a crucial role to play in designing effective programs and documenting their success. The job is demanding and sometimes heartwrenching. But just imagine if the next national incidence study were to document a sharp *decrease* in the rate of maltreatment. Each project, whatever its scope, is trying to make that fantasy a reality—of stopping the pain before it starts. Those of us engaged in child abuse prevention recognize that not only are the children our future, we are theirs.

## References

Aber, J. L., Allen, J. P., Carlson, V., & Cicchetti, D. (1989). The effects of maltreatment on development during early childhood: Recent studies and their theoretical, clinical, and policy implications. In D. Cicchetti & V. Carlson (Eds.), *Child maltreatment: Theory and research on the causes and consequences of child abuse and neglect* (pp. 579-619). New York: Cambridge University Press.

Aber, J. L., & Cicchetti, D. (1984). Socioemotional development in maltreated children: An empirical and theoretical analysis. In H. Fitzgerald, B. Lester, & M. Yogman (Eds.), *Theory and research in behavioral pediatrics*. Vol. II (pp. 147-205). New York: Plenum.

Barnes, H. V., Goodson, B. D., & Layzer, J. I. (1995). *National evaluation of family support programs: Review of research on supportive interventions for children and families* (Contract No. 105-94-1925). Washington, DC: U.S. Department of Health and Human Services.

Belsky, J., & Vondra, J. (1989). Lessons from child abuse: the determinants of parenting. In D. Cicchetti & V. Carlson (Eds.), *Child maltreatment: Theory and research on the causes and consequences of child abuse and neglect* (pp. 153-202). New York: Cambridge University Press.

Beutler, L. E., Williams, R. A., & Zetzer, H. A. (1994). Efficacy of treatment for victims of child sexual abuse. *The Future of Children, 4* (2), 156-175.

Briere, J., & Elliott, D. M. (1994). Immediate and long-term impact of child sexual abuse. *The Future of Children, 4* (2), 54-69.

Bronfenbrenner, U. (1981). *The ecology of human development*. Cambridge, MA: Harvard University Press.

Cicchetti, D. (1989). How research on child maltreatment has informed the study of child development: perspectives from developmental psychopathology. In D. Cicchetti & V. Carlson, (Eds.), *Child maltreatment: Theory and research on the causes and consequences of child abuse and neglect* (pp. 377-431). New York: Cambridge University Press.

Cicchetti, D., & Carlson, V. (Eds.). (1989). *Child maltreatment: Theory and research on the causes and consequences of child abuse and neglect*. New York: Cambridge University Press.

Crouch, J. L., & Milner, J. S. (1993). Effects of child neglect on children. *Criminal Justice and Behavior, 20* (1), 49-65.

CSR, Inc. (1997). *Lessons learned: The experiences of nine child abuse and neglect prevention programs*. Available on-line at http://www.calib.com/nccanch.

Daro, D., & Gelles, R. (1992). Public attitudes and behaviors with respect to child abuse prevention. *Journal of Interpersonal Violence, 7*, 517-531.

English, D. (1998). The extent and consequences of child maltreatment. *The Future of Children, 8* (1), 39-53.

Erickson, M. F., Egeland, B., & Pianta, R. (1989). The effects of maltreatment on the development of young children. In D. Cicchetti & V. Carlson (Eds.), *Child maltreatment: Theory and research on the causes and consequences of child abuse and neglect* (pp. 647-684). New York: Cambridge University Press.

Feldman, K. W. (1997). Evaluation of physical child abuse. In M. E. Helfer, R. S. Kempe, & R. D. Krugman (Eds.), *The battered child* (pp. 175-220). Chicago: University of Chicago Press.

Fink, A., & McCloskey, L. (1990). Moving child abuse and neglect prevention programs forward: Improving program evaluations. *International Journal of Child Abuse and Neglect, 14,* 187-206.

Garbarino, J. (1976). A preliminary study of some ecological correlates of child abuse: The impact of socioeconomic stress on mothers. *Child Development, 47,* 178-185.

Garbarino, J., & Sherman, D. (1980). High-risk neighborhoods and high-risk families: The human ecology of child maltreatment. *Child Development, 51,* 188-198.

Giles-Sims, S. J. (1985). A longitudinal study of battered children of battered wives. *Family Relations, 43,* 205-210.

Hartman, C. R., & Burgess, A. W. (1989). Sexual abuse of children: Causes and consequences. In D. Cicchetti & V. Carlson (Eds.), *Child maltreatment: Theory and research on the causes and consequences of child abuse and neglect* (pp. 95-128). New York: Cambridge University Press.

Kaufman, J., & Zigler, E. (1987). Do abused children become abusive parents? *American Journal of Orthopsychiatry, 57,* 186-192.

Kempe, R. S. (1997). A developmental approach to the treatment of abused children. In M. E. Helfer, R. S. Kempe, & R. D. Krugman (Eds.), *The battered child* (pp. 543-565). Chicago: University of Chicago Press.

Kitzman, H., Olds, D. L., Henderson, C. R., Hanks, C., Cole, R., Tatelbaum, R., McConnochie, K. M., Sidora, K., Luckey, D. W., Shaver, D., Engelhardt, K., James, D., & Barnard, K. (1997). Effects of prenatal and infancy home visitation by nurses on pregnancy outcomes, childhood injuries, and repeated childbearing: A randomized controlled trial. *Journal of the American Medical Association, 278,* 644-652.

McCurdy, K., & Daro, D. (1994). Child maltreatment: A national survey of reports and fatalities. *Journal of Interpersonal Violence, 9,* 75-94.

McKay, M. M. (1994). The link between domestic violence and child abuse: Assessment and treatment considerations. *Child Welfare, 73,* 29-39.

National Clearinghouse on Child Abuse and Neglect Information. (1997a). *Child abuse statistics.* Available on-line at http://www.calib.com/nccanch.

National Clearinghouse on Child Abuse and Neglect Information. (1997b). *In Fact...Answers to frequently asked questions on child abuse and neglect.* Available on-line at http://www.calib.com/nccanch/pubs/infact.htm.

National Clearinghouse on Child Abuse and Neglect Information. (1997c). *National child abuse and neglect statistical fact sheet.* Available on-line at http://www.calib.com/nccanch/pubs/stats.htm.

National Clearinghouse on Child Abuse and Neglect Information. (1997d). *What is child maltreatment?* Available on-line at http://www.calib.com/nccanch/pubs/whatis.htm.

National Research Council. (1993). *Understanding child abuse and neglect.* Washington, DC: National Academy Press.

Olds, L. D. (1983). An intervention program for high-risk families. In R. Hoekelman (Ed.), *A round table on minimizing high-risk parenting* (pp. 247-268). Media, PA: Harwal Publishing Co.

Olds, D. L., & Henderson, C. R. (1989). The prevention of maltreatment. In D. Cicchetti & V. Carlson (Eds.), *Child maltreatment: Theory and research on the causes and consequences of child abuse and neglect* (pp. 722-763). New York: Cambridge University Press.

Olds, D., Kitzman, H., Cole, R., & Robinson, J. (1997). Theoretical foundations of a program of home visitation for pregnant women and parents of young children. *Journal of Community Psychology, 25,* 9-25.

Polansky, N., Chalmers, M. A., Buttenwieser, E., & Williams, D. P. (1981). *Damaged parents: An anatomy of child neglect.* Chicago: University of Chicago Press.

Reichert, S. K. (1997). Medical evaluation of the sexually abused child. In M. E. Helfer, R. S. Kempe, & R. D. Krugman (Eds.), *The battered child* (pp. 313-328). Chicago: University of Chicago Press.

Ricciuti, H. N., & Dorman, R. (1983). Interaction of multiple factors contributing to high-risk parenting. In R. A. Hoekelman (Ed.), *Minimizing high-risk parenting* (pp. 187-210). Media, PA: Harwal Publishing.

Sedlak, A. J., & Broadhurst, D. D. (1996). *Third national incidence study of child abuse and neglect: Final report.* Washington, DC: U.S. Government Printing Office for the U.S. Department of Health and Human Services.

U.S. Department of Health and Human Services, National Center on Child Abuse and Neglect [DHHS]. (1996a*). Child abuse and neglect case-level data 1993: Working paper 1.* Washington, DC: U.S. Government Printing Office.

U.S. Department of Health and Human Services [DHHS], National Center of Child Abuse and Neglect. (1996b). *Child Abuse Prevention and Treatment Act, As Amended.* 42 U.S.C. §101 et seq; 42 USC §116 et seq. ACF Regulations: 45 CFR 1340. Washington, DC: U. S. Government Printing Office.

U.S. Department of Health and Human Services [DHHS]. (1997). *Child maltreatment 1995: Reports from the states to the National Child Abuse and Neglect Data System.* Washington, DC: U.S. Government Printing Office.

Widom, C. S. (1992). *The cycle of violence.* Washington, DC: National Institute of Justice.

Zigler, E., & Hall, N. W. (1989). Physical child abuse in America: Past, present, and future. In D. Cicchetti & V. Carlson (Eds.), *Child maltreatment: Theory and research on the causes and consequences of child abuse and neglect* (pp. 38-75). New York: Cambridge University Press.

# Cultural Competence: Communicating Effectively

Every prevention project is an effort to communicate. Prevention programs try to communicate the benefits of adopting alternative, positive ways of thinking, doing, and perceiving as a substitute for the behaviors and attitudes associated with maltreatment. Learning how to perceive and respond appropriately when confronted by cultural differences is critical if the project is going to persuade others to adopt the alternatives suggested by the program. Therefore, developing cultural competence is a basic prerequisite for working in the field of child abuse and neglect prevention.

Cultivating a knowledge of other ways of thinking and responding, combined with knowing how to show respect for others who are different from yourself, is the foundation of cultural competence. A lack of awareness of accepted norms can easily sabotage a project's efforts by miscommunication and by unintentionally offending the target popu-

**23**

lation. It is beyond the scope of this chapter to provide a detailed description of various cultural groups. (For culture-specific information, see Lee & Richardson [1991] and Locke [1992].) Rather, the intent is to provide basic principles to follow that will assist you in developing cultural competence.

When working with people of a different culture, effective communication results when a conscious effort is made to understand others and build a rapport with them. Each culture has a unique style of communication based on what is customary, traditional, or functional in that culture.

# How Is Cultural Competence Developed?

A prevention project achieves cultural competence when staff generate attitudes and policies that help them work effectively with members of other cultures, when they are skilled in interpreting cultural cues and attentive to cultural differences, and when the agency adapts and monitors services to meet participants' needs. Listed below are some characteristics of cultural competence.

★ Attitudes are open and unbiased.

★ Policies are flexible and culturally neutral.

★ Practices are in tune with the culture of the participants or clients.

Multicultural development, as described by Pedersen [1988], is a continuous learning process based on three stages of development: awareness, knowledge, and skills.

## *Awareness*

★ Ability to recognize different and indirect (nonverbal) communication styles

★ Awareness and interest in cultural and linguistic differences

★ Sensitivity to the myths and stereotypes of the culture

★ Concern for the welfare of persons from another culture

★ Ability to articulate elements of his or her own culture

★ Awareness of the relationships between cultural groups

## Knowledge

★ The culture (history, traditions, values, family systems, and artistic expressions) of clients

★ The impact of clients and ethnicity on behavior (particularly help-seeking behavior), attitudes, and values

★ The role of language, speech patterns, and communication styles in various cultures

★ The culture-specific resources (agencies, persons, informal helping networks, and research) that can be utilized on behalf of clients and communities

★ The ways that professional values may conflict with or accommodate the clients' needs and values

★ The impact of social service policies and power relationships in the community, agencies, or institutions on clients from various cultural groups

## Skills

★ Knows techniques for learning about cultures

★ Communicates accurate information on behalf of clients and their communities

★ Openly discusses racial and ethnic differences and issues and responds to culturally based cues

★ Assesses the meaning of ethnicity for individual clients

★ Differentiates between the symptoms of intrapsychic stress and stress arising from cultural differences

★ Uses resources on behalf of clients and their communities

★ Recognizes and combats racism in individuals and institutions

★ Evaluates the validity and applicability of new techniques, research, and knowledge for work with ethnic minorities

Cultural competence matures as certain values become internalized. These values are presented as part of the findings of a project sponsored by the National Institute of Mental Health, Child and Adolescent Service System Program (CASSP) in the monograph, *Towards a Culturally Competent System of Care* [Cross et al. 1989]. The common values that project staff should develop in becoming culturally competent include the following:

★ Understanding the effects that negative historical and current experiences have had on minorities—such as annihilation, slavery, internment camps, oppression, discrimination, prejudice, and racism

★ Respecting the unique, culturally defined needs of the target population

★ Acknowledging culture as a major force in shaping behaviors, values, and social behavior

★ Viewing the family, community, church, or traditionally respected individuals as important sources of support for minority populations

★ Starting with the "family," as defined by each culture, as the first point of intervention

★ Recognizing that the concepts of "family" and "community" are different for various cultures and even for subgroups within cultures

★ Functioning with the awareness that the dignity of the person is not guaranteed unless the dignity of his/her people is preserved

★ Understanding that clients are best served by persons who are part of or are in tune with the clients' own culture

★ Respecting the family as the means of understanding the individual and as the primary support for individuals

★ Recognizing that thought patterns should be equally valued and may influence how a person views problems and solutions

★ Respecting cultures that may value traditional processes in doing things

★ Recognizing that people from minority groups are dealing with bicultural issues that may affect behaviors and adjustments

## How Can a Project Build in the Ability to Relate Effectively to People of Different Cultures?

Any prevention program working with specific ethnic or minority populations should recruit and/or train staff who can work effectively with the target population. The program administrators can do several things to foster cultural competence:

★ When hiring staff, carefully weigh academic training along with cultural competence as criteria for delivering program services. It is possible that cultural competence is more important for some projects than advanced education.

★ Include questions about cultural experience and attitudes in the interviewing process: "Have you had experiences with cultures different from your own? What was the experience like for you?" Do not take a response such as, "Oh, I can work with all types of people" at face value. It may be that an individual is unaware of her own limitations regarding cultural competence. Look for clues that note openness and an ability to relate, without bias or negative feelings regarding the experience.

★ Provide training to staff on cultural issues and methods of working effectively with members of different cultures, including the culture of poverty.

★ Provide both workshop and on-site experiences. Reward those who work toward developing cultural competence.

★ Provide opportunities for staff to recognize and resolve conflicts in professional values versus ethnic values, or to recognize and work out personal stereotypes, biases, or prejudices. Workshops and videotapes are beneficial. (See the Resources section at the end of the chapter for information on ordering the videos "Cultural Identity Development" and "Color Blind.")

★ Be attentive to staff "cliques" that develop along racial or ethnic lines. Attempt to integrate staff through informal gatherings, as well as formal trainings.

★ Provide information about how a person in a specific culture generally reports or reacts to stress and crisis, as well as information about the culture's language, speech patterns, roles, rituals, help-seeking behaviors, family structure, and subgroup differences. Ask those who are knowledgeable about a given culture for assistance.

★ Discuss issues of power and different perceptions of power, especially as they relate to the helping relationship. Keep in mind that some cultural groups do not value hierarchy or one authority figure, but rather the importance of contribution by all persons involved with a particular process.

★ Teach interviewing and communication techniques that are sensitive to and respect cultural differences. Be well informed regarding communication styles. Make special efforts in cases where more than one language is spoken.

★ Hold programs in neighborhoods that are comfortable and familiar to the participants. Settings must be nonthreatening and not carry a stigma of association (e.g., areas known for racial prejudice or extensive drug or criminal activities are not good choices).

★ Include the input, opinions, and suggestions of participants into all stages of the project. Work with the power structure of influential persons in the ethnic community. Ask for help.

★ Provide training about the history, traditions, values, and other unique factors about a minority group. Make sure that professionals understand that *all* cultures have made significant contributions to the world. Encourage professionals to read magazines and newspapers published by different groups.

★ Locate and use existing community resources that are culturally aware. Be sure that all program participants will feel at ease in using the community resources.

★ Design the intervention to take into account such specific cultural information as language and customs. Make sure pictures or photographs of people in written materials show individuals from the cultural or racial groups you are serving.

## Cultural Differences and Child Maltreatment

While cultural competence is important for all "helping professionals," there is additionally complexity to working with families of various cultural backgrounds on the issue of child maltreatment. As Korbin states, "The challenge in understanding child maltreatment from the vantage point of different cultures is to encompass cultural diversity and to ensure equitable standards of care and protection for all children" [Korbin 1997, p. 29].

Cultural competence does not mean that we ignore child protection laws or the impact of certain practices upon children's growth and development simply because that practice occurs in a given culture. As Korbin further states, "It is important to recognize that cultural practices are not necessarily benign simply because they are cultural"

[Korbin 1997, p. 31]. Therefore, when a cultural practice collides with state definitions of abuse or neglect, it cannot be ignored or excused.

It is also misguided to attribute abusive or neglectful practices to a cultural difference simply because the family belongs to a certain racial or cultural group. It is a red flag for a staff person to say, "That's OK, because that's just the way *those people* treat their kids."

In some instances, parents may need to be educated regarding state law and/or the impact of a specific practice upon their child. There are instances in which individuals from other cultures can hold views of a certain child-rearing practice that are diametrically opposite from yours. And some cultures may consider mainstream American child-rearing practices to be abusive! For example, pediatricians in the United States encourage parents to place infants in their own beds and rooms for the night. Many cultures view this practice as detrimental to social development and even potentially dangerous [Korbin 1997].

The culturally competent professional will use her/his knowledge and skills to help families in a sensitive manner and never forget that a child's health and welfare must always be held paramount.

## References

Ahn, N. H., & Gilbert, N. (1992). Cultural diversity and sexual abuse prevention. *Social Service Review*, 411-427.

Brislin, R. W. (1988) Prejudice in intercultural communication. In L. A. Samovar & R. E. Porter (Eds.), *Intercultural communication: A reader* (5th ed.) (pp. 339-381). Belmont, CA: Wadsworth Publishing.

Brislin, R. W., Cushner, K., Cherrie, C., & Yong, M. (1986). *Intercultural interactions: A practice guide. Vol. 9: Cross-Cultural Research and Methodology Series*. Beverly Hills, CA: Sage Publications.

Cross, T. L., Bazron, B. J., Dennis, K. W., & Isaacs, M. R. (1989). *Towards a culturally competent system of care: A monograph on effective services for minority children who are severely emotionally disturbed*. Available from Child and Adolescent Service System Program, Technical Assistance Center, Georgetown University Child Development Center, 3800 Reservoir Road, N.W., Washington, DC 20007.

Fitchen, J. M. (1981). *Poverty in rural America: A case study.* Boulder, CO: Westview Press, Inc.

Gallegos, J. S. (1984). The ethnic competence model for social work education. In B. W. White (Ed.), *Color in a white society* (pp. 1-9). Silver Spring, MD: National Association of Social Workers.

Kochman, T. (1981). *Black and white: Styles in conflict.* Chicago: University of Chicago Press.

Korbin, J. E. (Ed.). (1981). *Child abuse and neglect: Cross-cultural perspectives.* Berkeley, CA: University of California Press.

Korbin, J. E. (1997). Culture and child maltreatment. In M. E. Helfer, R. S. Kempe, & R. D. Krugman (Eds.), *The battered child* (pp. 29-48). Chicago: University of Chicago Press.

McWhirter, J. J., & Ryan, C. A. (1991). Counseling the Navajo: Cultural understanding. *Journal of Cultural Counseling and Development, 19*(2), 74-82.

Pedersen, P. (1988). *A handbook for developing cultural awareness.* Alexandria, VA: American Association for Counseling and Development.

Pinderhughes, E. E. (1991). The delivery of child welfare services to African American clients. *American Orthopsychiatric Association, 61*(4), 599-605.

Pinderhughes, E. B. (1979, July 24). Teaching empathy in cross-cultural social work. *Social Work,* 312-316.

Ponterotto, G. J., Rieger P. B., Barrett, A., & Sparks, R. (1994). Assessing multicultural competence: A review of instrumentation. *Journal of Counseling & Development, 72,* 316-322

Rodwell, K. M., & Blankebaker, A., (1992) Strategies for developing cross-cultural sensitivity: Wounding as metaphor. *Journal of Social Work Education, 28* (2), 153-165.

Sue, D.W., Bernier, Y., Durran, A., Feinberg, L., Pederson, P. B., Smith, E. J., & Vasquez-Nuttal, E. (1982). Position paper: Cross-cultural counseling competencies. *The Counseling Psychologist, 10,* 45-52.

Sue, D.W., Arredondo, P., & McDavis, R. J. (1992). Cultural counseling competencies and standards: A call to the profession. *Journal of Cultural Counseling and Development, 20*(2), 64-88.

# Resources for Training in Cultural Competence

Allen, T., & Vendelande, M. "Color blind" [video]. Cleveland, OH: WEWS-Channel 5. Available from Classic Video, 5001 East Royalton Road, Cleveland, Ohio 44147; telephone 410/838-5377; *http://www.classicworldwide.com*; e-mail dubs@classicworldwide.com.

Lee, C. C., & Richardson, B. (Eds.). (1991). *Cultural issues in counseling: New approaches to diversity.* Alexandria, VA: American Association for Counseling and Development.

Locke, D. C. (1992). *Increasing cultural understanding: A comprehensive model.* Newbury Park, CA: Sage Publications.

People of Color Leadership Institute, 714 G Street, SE, Suite A, Washington, DC 20003; telephone: 202/544-3144; fax: 202/547-3601.

Solomon, C., & Jackson-Jobe, P. (1992). *Helping homeless people: Unique challenges and solutions.* Alexandria, VA: American Association for Counseling and Development.

Stack, B. C. (1975). *All our kin: strategies for survival in a black community.* New York: Harper & Row.

Stevenson, K. M., Cheung, K. M., & Leung, P. (1992). A new approach to training child protective services workers for ethnically sensitive practice. *Child Welfare, 71* (4), 291-305.

Sue, D. W. (1992). "Cultural identity development" [video]. North Amherst, MA: Microtraining Associates, Inc. Available from Microtraining Associates, Inc., Box 9641, North Amherst, MA 01059-9641; telephone: 413/549-2630; fax: 413/549-0212.

# Determining Community Needs

**3**

## In this chapter ...

A properly planned and executed needs assessment provides the necessary information for making important project decisions. The following basic needs assessment steps establish the foundation for developing sound project design and for effective project implementation:

★ Determine the goal(s) of the needs assessment

★ Identify and describe the target population

★ Describe the needs of the target population and the possible solutions to meet the needs

★ Assess the needs and list them as priorities in order of importance

★ Communicate the results to decisionmakers

A variety of needs assessment approaches are available to suit the individual assessment requirements of any project:

★ Statistical approaches

★ Opinion-oriented approaches

★ Combinations of several approaches

Having an idea to do something about child maltreatment is the first step in initiating a prevention program. The next step is gathering the evidence to support that idea and creating a feasible and focused program. Developing a prevention idea into a viable program requires decisionmaking. For example, a project must decide what types of maltreatment to prevent, what population to target, and what services to provide. To make these decisions and prudently direct the focus of a project, it is important to have the right information. A needs assessment is just the tool for doing this. (See box on page 34.)

Such an assessment collects information from various sources about the needs of people in the community and the services available to meet those needs. The

## What Can a Needs Assessment Do?

★ Indicate the gap between the number of persons who have a problem and the number who are getting help for that problem.

★ Reveal the number of people who fit particular described conditions.

★ Reveal the number of people who might be at risk of maltreatment (e.g., victims or perpetrators).

★ Identify barriers that may be preventing those who need services from receiving services.

★ Indicate the geographic areas and the numbers of persons in those areas that are at risk.

★ Identify groups of persons who are relatively similar in their need for services but are not receiving them.

★ Tell how a community compares (similar or different) to other communities in numbers or types of at-risk persons.

★ Indicate people's level of knowledge about maltreatment issues and available services.

★ Tell what other agencies or programs are providing services and the kinds of services provided.

★ Explore people's beliefs, attitudes, and feelings about child abuse and neglect issues and services.

★ Identify people's suggestions for services.

★ Satisfy requirements of funding sources by providing facts and figures.

★ Provide baseline data to show change or improvement when compared with project outcomes.

★ Change vague perceptions into facts that authenticate and define the "need."

★ Generate community awareness and draw attention to the need for legislative or policy action.

information is used to make decisions about how to design a project to meet the needs that are not already being met. However, the results of the assessment require careful analysis and interpretation before being used for making decisions.

# Preparing for the Needs Assessment

## *Gathering Background Information*

Anyone planning to do a prevention project should have familiarity with some basic information on maltreatment, but it is not necessary to become an expert. Some basic library research, combined with information available from federal agencies and national organizations, provides both an academic and practical perspective on the problem. Most national resources now have websites and many have on-line documents that you can download and print. (See Appendixes B and C for a listing of resources.)

Background knowledge and information about the following topics is most useful:

★ The types of abuse and definitions

★ Research findings about the causes of abuse

★ Types of interventions

★ Family dynamics

★ Child development stages

★ Indicators of abuse

★ Cultural differences

★ Urban/rural characteristics

★ Study findings and statistics and their implications

★ Implications of poverty on lifestyle

★ Effects of stress on parenting quality

## Defining the Scope of the Needs Assessment

Before doing a needs assessment, investigate whether another agency or project has recently conducted a needs assessment that satisfies your requirements and whether they will make the findings available. If this is not an option, then consider the availability of the following resources:

★ **Time:** Is there a timetable or deadline for the needs assessment (i.e., when is the proposal due?)?

★ **Money:** What is the budget for the needs assessment?

★ **Staff:** Can the staff perform the assessment? Is outside expertise needed? Can volunteers be used?

If resources are limited, investigate the possibility of combining efforts in a joint needs assessment with another agency or project. See Case #1 for an example of working with limited resources.

### Case #1: Working with Limited Resources

An agency decides to apply for funding to do a prevention project, because agency staff have observed a need for a teen parent education program, and a number of teen parent abuse cases have been referred to the agency. The application deadline for a local funder is six weeks away. Staff hold a meeting to devise a timeline for doing a needs assessment and to consider budget and staff resources.

The agency realizes that it must provide concrete evidence to show that a teen parent education program is needed. It must have the results within three weeks to allow itself time to develop a proposal.

Because of the limited time and limited budget, it is decided that a mailed key informant survey is possible using a modified survey developed for another project. The survey will determine whether other such programs exist and whether there is community support for a new one. Using an existing list of agency contacts, staff create a list of key informants and gatekeepers in the community. The mailing of the survey will be followed up by direct phone contact to ensure the quick return of the survey. Allowing three weeks for the mailing and return of the survey leaves three weeks to develop a proposal.

An agency staff person is assigned to collect recent maltreatment incidence rates for teen parents in the community from the local child protective service. Agency statistics from files showing evidence of maltreatment to children by teen parents are also compiled. After the information is collected, it is analyzed and indeed shows a need and support for teen parent education. The agency decides to focus the program on developing positive parenting skills.

The combination of all the needs assessment information from the three sources supplies enough evidence for the purposes of this particular project proposal.

# Doing the Needs Assessment

The following section contains five steps to use as guidelines in doing a needs assessment. We have also provided a variety of different project scenarios as case examples to illustrate these steps.

## Step 1. Determine the Goal(s) of the Needs Assessment

The needs assessment may have one or more goals. For instance, the results may be used 1) in a project proposal, 2) as baseline data for evaluation purposes, or 3) to make decisions for long-term agency planning. It is important to start with clear goals for the needs assessment. To determine the goals, identify *how* the assessment results will be applied, as well as *who* will be using the results. Based on the goals, choose different needs assessment approaches to obtain the information that will help to make decisions about reaching your goals. (See Case #2 and Case #3.)

### Case #2: One Set of Data Meets Two Goals

A community group wants information to establish a need for parent education for parents of preschool children in day care settings and to serve as the basis for a project proposal. They also want information that will be able to show any effect the program has in reducing a potentially maltreating behavior or attitude. The goals of the assessment are to collect information for 1) establishing a needs statement for a proposal and 2) to provide baseline data for program evaluation.

In this case, a standardized test could be administered as a pretest to measure specific behaviors or attitudes before the parent education program begins. The pretest scores serve as an indicator of the need for parent education in the designated preschool. The same data can then be compared to posttest results obtained when parent classes are completed to assess program effectiveness.

## Case #3: Collecting Different Types of Data

An agency wants to establish an adult training program about child maltreatment. The planners want information about the extent of the need and interest within the community for the training program. They also want to know if such a training program should be designed to cover a broad or narrow range of topics or if the program should be planned as a package of several trainings over a longer period of time. In addition, staff want information about training topics, scheduling preferences, and the possibility of charging a fee for the training.

The goals of the assessment are to collect information for 1) establishing a need for a training program; 2) determining the extent and length of time the need must be serviced; and 3) determining the topics, times, and fees for marketing the program. Outlined below is the plan to satisfy their information needs and the plan's results.

### Who will use the assessment results?

An agency planning to provide training programs on the topic of child maltreatment.

### How will the results be applied?

The goals of the assessment are to collect information regarding the following:

- The need for the training program
- The geographical area(s) to concentrate on if the training program is widely needed
- The type of audience most likely to request a training
- An estimate of the number of expected requests there will be for the training
- The training topics most likely to be requested

### Assessment Method

- Mail a survey to a sample of potential groups who may want the training. The survey sample is selected carefully to represent a variety of groups and locations who may be interested in the training. The survey is designed to find out the following:

  - The group's level of knowledge about child abuse, parenting skills, child development, or the specific topic the project is focusing on

  - The numbers who would attend

  - The topics that the group would be most interested in hearing about

  - Scheduling preference (length of presentation, day, time of day, month, etc.)

  - A description of the group (socioeconomic and demographic checklist)

  - Willingness to pay for the training

- Have the potential trainers complete a questionnaire covering the following:

  - Areas of expertise

  - Times available for presenting

  - Content of presentation

### Assessment Results

- Eighty percent of the schools in urban and rural areas were interested in the training. The rural areas had the least access to any training resources. Sixty percent of the other groups surveyed who worked with children, such as YMCAs and church groups, were also interested in training.

- The topic areas most requested were learning about indicators of abuse, reporting abuse, and referral for services.

- Scheduling preferences were predominantly after-school hours for schools and a variety of preferences for other groups.

- Participants in school trainings would be 75% professional and paraprofessionals and 25% volunteers and parents. Other groups would have more than 50% nonprofessional participants.

- The urban schools and groups accounted for 85% of the potential training requests; however, rural areas expressed a greater need.

- The preference for content and level of content of the topics varied in line with the group's level of professional experience in working with children.

- Ninety percent of the urban schools had some discretionary budgeted funds to pay a minimum fee for the training. Forty-five percent of the rural schools would be able to pay for the training. Only 15% of the other groups had money available for a training fee.

## Step 2. Identify and Describe the Target Population

If the target population is not clearly identified, then the needs assessment may help in identifying the target population. In some cases, the target population may already be identified in a general way (e.g., teen mothers), but then the needs assessment describes and defines the target population more precisely (e.g., teen mothers aged 13-15 years living in this county). This is especially valuable in estimating and deciding on the numbers of persons the project can actually serve.

Target populations may be individuals, couples, families, or larger groups such as neighborhoods or schools. Before defining the target population, you should take into account the program resources, the size of the potential target population and other factors. For example, one consideration might be recruiting enough volunteers to work with participants. Demographic characteristics, such as age, sex, income, and marital status, as well as other problems and conditions (e.g., substance abuse history) are used to clearly define who will be served by the project. Case #4 clearly designates the target population.

### Case #4: Describing the Target Population

The **Parenting Exceptional Children Project**, a parent support program located in Cuyahoga County, Ohio, defined the target population as all 45 mothers of preschool children who were developmentally disabled and attending a county early intervention program. The program taught stress management and parenting skills specific to the needs of these special children.

## *Using Different Methods to Identify the Target Population*

There are a number of ways to designate the target population. Outlined below are some suggested methods.

★ Perform a literature search to find research data regarding possible populations.

★ Interview experts or agency administrators and service providers who work with these populations.

★ Obtain local statistics (numbers, rates, socioeconomic descriptors) from public and/or private agencies.

★ Send a survey to key informants (i.e., people who know the target population and/or services) to find out about the available existing services in the community, eligibility to receive services, and actual use of services.

Case #5 illustrates how a statewide public awareness campaign determined who to target and how to deliver their message.

### *Case #5: Who Is the Real Target Population?*

Initially, **South Carolina Cares** (a statewide prevention initiative) wanted to target parents who abused their children. During initial meetings, the group identified two guiding objectives for the public awareness and public relations campaign:

• Increase the public's understanding of the relationship between substance abuse and child maltreatment and inform the public on how to access help in the local communities.

• Assist families and children involved with child and substance abuse in finding help in their local communities through a 24-hour information and referral service established under the project.

In an effort to verify their assumption about the target audience, the group conducted focus groups and interviews and gathered information from the South Carolina Household Survey. Project staff discovered that enablers (individuals such as grandparents, neighbors, clergy, or friends who know that a person is abusing his/her child) were in the best position, and indicated a willingness, to report incidents of child abuse and neglect.

The research indicated that abusive parents would be a difficult group to reach, and if parents were reached, there would be little success in affecting their behavior. Based upon analysis of the research, the group decided to switch their focus from abusing parents to enablers.

The research also indicated that the campaign would be more successful if a regional approach were developed. Since South Carolina has distinct regions with particular nuances, the campaign would reach more people if particular public service announcements had a regional flavor to them.

# Step 3. Describe the Needs of the Target Population and the Possible Solutions

The population's needs must be clearly defined and matched to appropriate solutions. Use a variety of data to document a need. Information should include how the need will be reduced by the project.

Case #6 illustrates how one project obtained research information from the literature, combined that information with local statistical data, built a substantial case, and documented a population's need. The intervention chosen by the project relates closely to the assessed need.

### Case #6: Matching Needs and Interventions

The **Young Moms and Dads Program**, in Wood County, Ohio, developed its prevention program to reduce the problem of maltreatment experienced by children of adolescent parents. The program made use of data reported in the *Journal of Adolescent Health Care* [Panzarine 1988]. The data showed that adolescent parents are less sensitive to their infant's needs, use less verbal communication with their infant, and show less eye contact, smiling, and physical contact with their infant. Also, the data showed that adolescents are less positive about parenting, more critical of their children, and use more physical punishment than older parents.

Additional statistics obtained from the county health department provided the number of adolescent parents in the county, their current school status, and social service treatment numbers to support the designation of at-risk.

The Young Moms and Dads Program incorporated parent education and parent support interventions that were previously shown to improve adolescent interactions with their children and enhanced the child's development.

Following is a detailed description of the assessment methods and results obtained by the Young Moms and Dads Program. The assessment was designed to describe the needs of the target population so that an intervention could be chosen to meet those needs.

### ★ Assessment Questions

- What are the needs of the adolescent parents?

- What should the project offer adolescent parents to help deal with their needs and problems?

### ★ Assessment Objective

The project planners wanted information about the following:

- Whether teens lack necessary social supports as adolescents and as parents

- Whether adolescent parents need to learn about child development, positive nurturing behaviors, and positive parenting skills

- Whether other supports may be needed, such as child care or transportation

- Whether adolescent parents may need counseling

### ★ Assessment Method

- Review the literature to find successful interventions with this population or a similar one.

- Collect data and statistics from a previous agency pilot of this program (e.g., records of attendance, demographic information, descriptions of families).

- Survey, by means of a personal interview, a number of key informants from across the county about their insights regarding this population and about available existing services and costs, eligibility to receive services, and actual use of services for this population.

★ **Assessment Results**

- Providing parent education combined with parent support services was a successful method in working with adolescent parents to reduce child maltreatment.

- Certain methods of working with adolescents had better results than others.

- Adolescent parents showed a need for information about all areas of parenting, as well as about coping with adolescence.

- The assessment yielded specific information:

  • Parents were at high risk for maltreatment and communicated less with their baby if the baby had complications at birth. Therefore, the program starts working with parents while they are still in the hospital after delivery.

  • Mothers spend more time interacting positively and playing with their baby if the father is involved with the baby as well. Therefore, the program now encourages fathers who are involved parents to become a part of the program.

## Step 4. Assess the Needs and List Them as Priorities in Order of Importance

Prioritizing needs is one of the most difficult decisions that project planners have to make. The decision must be based on the results from the needs assessment, as well as realistic budgets and time frames. The needs as perceived by the target population, the funder, and the project planners must also be evaluated and balanced.

Possible prioritizing criteria include the following:

★ The funder's preferred interests

★ Budget and time frame

★ Level of staff expertise or experience

★ Availability of other resources (e.g., volunteer time, equipment, etc.)

★ Willingness of target population to participate

Case #7 describes a project that had multiple needs to meet, as well as a number of barriers to overcome.

## Case #7: Prioritizing and Meeting Multiple Needs

The **Hispanic Family Education Project**, based in northeastern Ohio, promoted awareness of child abuse and neglect issues and prevention through the media and through contact with the community. The program targeted migrant and seasonal farmworker families in northwest and northeast Ohio and the rural Hispanic population. This project's needs assessment described the target population and its most critical needs, as well as what prevention methods would best address those needs. It was also useful in prioritizing needs.

### Assessment Questions

• Which needs are most critical to the target population?

• How can the project meet those needs?

### Assessment Objectives

• Determine the greatest need of the target population.

• Get an estimate of the size of the target population.

• Establish a list of barriers that must be overcome in reaching the target population.

• Identify specialized skills and expertise the staff must have to work with the target population.

• Identify possible assistance from other cooperative programs or agencies.

• Identify the amount and availability of Hispanic and/or bilingual materials.

### Assessment Methods

- A meeting was held to brainstorm with Hispanic staff and other experts in the community to discuss the needs of the population and possible methods of reaching the population with the prevention message. (See **Tool #1, Structured Group Techniques**, for guidelines in conducting this type of meeting.)

- Several state and national projects were contacted to find out what prevention programs or agencies may be able to cooperate or offer specialized skills or bilingual or Hispanic materials. These contacts in turn referred them to other sources for materials.

- Key informants and agency personnel working on overlapping projects were contacted to find out if services or materials might be available.

### Assessment Results

- There is a wide disparity in estimates of the size of this population.

- Because of poverty, transience, language, and educational barriers, the target population has little or no awareness about maltreatment issues and little exposure to prevention messages or information.

- There is a scarcity of known, available bilingual and Hispanic materials, and the ones that were available from a number of local and national agencies and programs were insufficient to meet the need of this population.

- The use of media, in the form of posters and billboards, would be a good method of communicating basic prevention messages and informing the population of other sources of information. (It was decided not to use extensive written materials and TV messages, as they would have only limited success due to socioeconomic and literacy factors.)

- Having a bilingual/bicultural staff is essential.

- Distributing information and establishing contact with the target population can be accomplished by providing information points (booths) at events or places the population would be likely to attend.

- Other agencies and projects had materials or related services that could be used for distribution (e.g., bilingual or Hispanic pamphlets on health, marriage, education, etc.; a "Bookmobile" that could make available informational materials).

The project prioritized the needs it could realistically address successfully with its budget and staff. Increasing this population's general awareness of maltreatment was deemed a priority. It was decided that prevention information and other parenting and health information related to good child-rearing practices could best be communicated by means of a media campaign. Newly developed bilingual materials were given out at display booths and presentations at health fairs and community events that attracted numbers of the target population (i.e, "Farm Worker Days"). Also, high-impact messages would be displayed on Spanish language billboards placed along routes heavily traveled by the population, along with bilingual posters with short prevention messages.

Providing one-on-one contact through outreach workers, another identified need, was postponed as a need to be addressed in the future when more project resources were available.

## Step 5. Communicate the Results to Decisionmakers or Others Who Will Use the Results

Communicating needs assessment findings through written, graphic, or oral presentations can be a significant means of gaining support and funding for a proposed prevention project. If the needs assessment is only aimed at producing data for a proposal, then follow the directions of the funder and the standard format that is described in Chapter 5.

If an independent report is required as documentation of the needs assessment results, it should be written in a clear, concise style; be attractively presented; and highlight the content of greatest interest. Avoid or clearly explain technical terms. Be informative and cover topics that interest the audience. The report should include these sections:

- Executive summary (brief, 1-2 pages)

- Assessment questions and methods

- Results

- Implications

See **Tool #2, Needs Assessment: Written Reports**, for more details on reporting findings.

# Needs Assessment Approaches

There are a number of needs assessment approaches or methodologies available to suit the individual information requirements of any project. The different assessment approaches range from simple to sophisticated; however, most can be adapted to fit the budget, level of expertise, and scope of a particular project. The approaches that are easiest to use or require only minimal assistance are presented in the following section. If more complicated or extensive assessment is required, we recommend that you consult an expert.

## Statistical Approaches

Data-oriented approaches generally collect data from public records and from the U.S. Census Bureau to reveal certain population characteristics. Then, the data are analyzed to determine which community areas warrant program services and also to spot trends or problems that are occurring in the population.

When resources are limited, the use of available statistics is a reliable and easy approach. Since there is an enormous quantity of statistical data available, it is important to select only the type and kind of information that is actually useful for project purposes. (See Appendix D for sources of statistical information.)

### Demographic Characteristics and Social Indicators

Demographic characteristics and social indicator statistics can provide information about community needs as a whole or focus on a specific subpopulation. Populations are described through numbers measuring the occurrence of characteristics or behaviors. These facts can be used to 1) identify target populations, 2) estimate the number of people within a target population, or 3) estimate the size of the target population within a limited geographic area. Local, state, and federal government statistics and reports are the most common sources of descriptive statistics of this type. When combined with other sources and forms of information, a picture of community needs emerges. See Tables 1 and 2 for more information about where to find these kind of data and what type of data are available.

Demographic and other statistics (e.g., child abuse reports) are a simple and inexpensive source of data. However, the interpretation of the numbers requires some caution as well as expertise. Factors like service availability and community composition must be considered in making interpretations about whether a population is at-risk. Social indicators and demographics may reveal problems, but do not show solutions. Therefore, these statistics are best used together with other assessment methods.

### Recommendations for Collecting Statistical Data

★ Restrict the collection of demographic characteristics and social indicators to those that are important for the assessment.

★ Try to obtain data covering a period of several years.

★ Obtain information on a variety of factors, occurrence rates, community history or trends.

### Using Contacts to Obtain Data

If the data you need are not published or on-line, but are available through an agency or organization (e.g., child protection agency, United Way, police department), then it is important to find a person who is willing to be of assistance in locating and selecting the best data for the project's purpose. Spend some time finding a good contact person. Call or write to the agency or institution that has the data you need and explain your reasons for wanting the information. Ask for a contact person to help you and make that person your ally. Let her or him know how she/he is helping to reduce child maltreatment and ask for

***Table 1. Sources for Data***

U.S. Census

State Children's Trust Fund

Local/state health department

Hospitals

Mental health departments

State/local departments of child protective services

Government and private websites

Legal systems

National advocacy organizations

County governments

**Note:** See Appendix D for a listing of on-line statistical data sources.

help in meeting or finding contacts in other agencies or institutions that could provide useful information.

## Opinion-Oriented Approaches

Opinion-oriented approaches ask people in the community what they think about child maltreatment problems. There are several methods of doing this. Among the most frequently used are the community forum, structured groups, the community survey, and the key informant survey.

### *Community Forum*

The community forum is an open town meeting set up to discuss child maltreatment problems in the community. It is a method of obtaining input from the general population. It also increases public awareness about the problem of child maltreatment.

Be aware that the community forum results will only reflect the input of those who attend and may not represent the feelings of the general public. Using the structured group techniques described below with the attendees will stimulate participation and contribution of ideas. Consult with someone who has experience in using these group tech-

### Table 2. Demographic Characteristics and Social Indicators

- Parent category: single, two-parent
- Residence: independent, with parents, guardian, foster home, institution, other
- Male/female
- Employment
- Birth date/age
- Income
- Religion
- Mental/physical limitations
- Ethnic group
- Medical or social service history
- School: in years or grade completed, degrees
- Social assistance, lunch program, etc.
- Juvenile, criminal record
- History of abuse/neglect
- Drug/alcohol use
- Geographical area of residence
- Number of children, ages, mental/physical challenges
- School system

niques before using them. The meeting may also raise public expectations for immediate solutions. Be advised that a community forum requires substantial coordination, and the forum and the agenda should be well publicized.

### Structured Groups

A structured group assembles concerned or involved lay or professional individuals to help identify needs and distinguish populations with needs. This is an alternative method of obtaining input and can supplement findings from other sources. Specific questions are given to the group to discuss, and the group can explore solutions and program proposals that may have originated from other sources (e.g., library research, demographic analysis).

Structured groups add qualitative information and insights to quantitative findings. They are frequently chosen as a means of generating ideas or forming a consensus. Interaction among the group members follows structured steps to encourage the participation of all the members of the group.

In needs assessment, these group techniques help identify community needs as perceived by community members, and also permit prioritization of needs already identified. This process encourages community ownership of and input into any subsequent program that evolves. See **Tool #1, Structured Group Techniques**, for more information on the steps and procedures in using structured groups.

### Community Survey

The community survey is used to identify the needs of the community by asking a sample of the community members for their perceptions regarding community child abuse and neglect problems and needs. A questionnaire is designed that covers the relevant topic areas, and it is administered by mail, telephone, or face-to-face.

A community survey provides information about community awareness of problems, services, barriers to receiving services, types of services wanted, and can also be used as a public relations tool. The information obtained through a community survey is best used together with information obtained from other sources for making decisions. Before selecting the community survey approach, consider the fact that, depending on the number of people you survey, it may be costly and time consuming. How much money and staff time to invest depends on the scope and importance of the project.

### Key Informant Survey

The key informant survey asks selected leaders or experts from the community for their opinions or suggestions regarding child maltreatment in the community. Program planners who have a prevention idea but need more information to become focused can benefit by contacting knowledgeable and influential community leaders or key informants. Using key informants as a source of initial input can save an enormous amount of work and time by focusing the assessment on gathering the right information. Also, these people are often the same persons who have to be approached later for support and advocacy.

★ *Key informants* are people who have knowledge of the community, its people, their needs, and the kinds and rates of services that are being delivered or received. Key informants may also be leaders, experts, or others with unique insights (e.g., teachers, doctors, nurses, local technical experts, civil servants, agency administrators, religious leaders). Frequently, key informants have a great deal of contact with a cross section of the local population and are familiar with ethnic groups, businesses or organizations, and conditions in an area. Key informants may also come from within the setting that you are assessing, such as the principal or nurse within a school. Sometimes they can simply be people highly respected by others in the target population, though they possess no formal title or position.

★ *Gatekeepers* are those persons in the community who can "make things happen." They are persons of power and influence in education, government, business, or community organizations, who can supply crucial information about how community systems operate.

A key informant survey asks persons who are likely to have the most accurate information and insights to answer questions about community maltreatment prevention needs. The survey also collects information about how well maltreatment problems are being handled and may increase community awareness about child maltreatment.

The actual survey can be conducted by mail, telephone, or through face-to-face interviews. The survey information is analyzed to help make decisions for prevention program planning. In addition, it informs community leaders and service professionals about maltreatment concerns and includes them as partners in finding solutions. Thus, it is a valuable public relations tool. However, a key informant survey should be used cautiously as it may include opinions as well as objective information. Several methods of conducting surveys are described below.

★ *Interviews*, especially face-to-face interviews, can obtain in-depth answers. It is particularly appropriate when surveying persons who have difficulty responding in other ways. Interviews require a trained interviewer and, if many interviews are planned, it can be expensive and time consuming.

★ *Mailed surveys* are a versatile method of gathering large samples of responses. Responses may be more candid if anonymous. Generally, low return rates of mailed surveys are to be expected and should be considered before selecting this method.

★ *Sampling*, or surveying only a representative portion of a population, requires expert assistance. Ask for help at a local university, college, or agency with this expertise. It is a good alternative if the population is large and resources are limited.

**Tool #3, Advantages and Disadvantages of Using Surveys**, and **Tool #4, Using Community Leaders as Resources**, offer more recommendations regarding obtaining information from community leaders and others.

In Table 3, the variables in these needs assessment approaches have been scored on a scale from low to high. Table 4 describes the different variables. Case #8 shows how assessment information can assist a project.

### Case #8: Using Assessment for Planning and Decisionmaking

The **Cambodian Abuse Prevention Project**, Franklin County, Ohio, operated through a grassroots agency that worked closely with the community. The project used several approaches as part of its assessment.

## Table 3. Overview of Resources and Utility Issues in the Selection of Needs Assessment Approaches

|  | Using Available Data | Community Forum | Community Survey | Key Informant Survey |
|---|---|---|---|---|
| Time | low | low | high | moderate |
| Money | low | low | high | low |
| Technical skills | low | low | moderate | moderate |
| Community involvement | low | high | high | high |
| Useability | high | moderate | moderate | high |
| Shelf life | moderate | low | moderate | moderate |
| Amount/variety of information produced | moderate | low | high | moderate |
| Generalizability | high | low | high | moderate |

## Table 4. Descriptions of Variables

| | |
|---|---|
| Time | Amount of time to complete task; completing task includes (where appropriate) sample selection, instrument application, data collection, and data analysis |
| Money | Cost to complete task, including staff time, supplies, printing, postage, computer time, etc. |
| Technical skills | Skill required to either organize, coordinate, and/or conduct task, and analyze results |
| Community involvement | Ability to involve citizens of local community in terms of helping to collect data, or to provide supplementary information to data previously obtained; opinions about community needs or problems and mental health services; to be a primary source of data |
| Useability | Information is readily understood by staff and board; individual pieces of information are easily extracted; information can be used for a variety of purposes |
| Shelf life | Approximate amount of time for which information is valid |
| Amount/variety of information | The volume/quantity of information obtained; variety of types of information obtained |
| Generalizabilty | Ability of information obtained to be applicable to the total population of a given area |

### Key Informants

Key informants who were directly connected to the community (i.e., the agency director and agency staff who were Cambodian) pooled their insights regarding the needs of the target population and the means of reaching that population.

Also, 15 specialists (key informants) were surveyed for information, opinion, and observation in a number of areas of expertise, such as Cambodian practices, attitudes, and family issues. Some specific results were applied to the selection of an intervention:

- The population was known to be reluctant to participate in public groups or sessions and distrusted outsiders due to political persecution experienced in the past.

- Approximately 98% of Cambodian population had access to a VCR in their homes.

### Other Assessment Techniques

- Agency caseload records were checked and showed that approximately 50% of the target population were illiterate in either their own language, in English, or both.

- Virtually 100% of Cambodian parents (living in Franklin County) practice corporal punishment as a means of disciplining their children.

### Determinations, Based on Assessment

- It is vital to understand and work within the cultural context of the target population in presenting prevention information.

- Staff working with the target population should be bilingual.

- Surveys and tests of the target population (e.g., pretest or baseline data) should be done in the home.

This assessment information helped the project decide to use a video as an intervention method acceptable to the target population. Furthermore, the project decided to develop a culturally aware video to present constructive alternatives to corporal punishment as a means of disciplining children.

**Note:** The project evaluation showed a remarkable success rate for viewing the video that was developed. Out of the original 106 pretested parents, 100 had viewed the video, along with uncounted members of their families.

## Use Community Leaders as Resources

Whatever approach is decided upon, making contacts in the community is of prime importance to the success of a program. In particular, having the backing of community leaders makes it easier to identify funding sources and approach them with credibility. This can be done through a key informant survey or more informally by simply talking with key individuals whose support will be helpful. Obtaining the involvement of decisionmakers or community leaders early on establishes a bond that lasts for the duration of the project.

It makes good sense to develop a network of support at an early stage in planning any prevention program. See **Tool #4, Using Community Leaders as Resources**, for more information on this topic.

## Needs Assessment Builds Confidence in Program Success

Determining community needs through assessment establishes quantitative and qualitative evidence in support of a project's proposal to reduce child maltreatment. Knowing that a program is designed to meet real, unmet needs is the critical first step to program success. It enables project designers to make critical decisions about the most economical and effective allocation of prevention resources. As a consequence, both the project designer(s) and the sponsor or funder of the project experience a raised level of confidence in the ability of the project to achieve its prevention goals.

The next chapter, "Designing a Child Abuse Prevention Project," reviews the groundwork for establishing a prevention program.

## References

Connors, T. D. (Ed.). (1980). *The nonprofit organization handbook*. New York: McGraw-Hill.

Hagedorn, H. J., Beck, K., Neubert, S. F., & Werlin, S. H. (1976). Needs assessment. In *A working manual of simple program evaluation techniques for community mental health centers*. Rockville, MD: National Institute for Mental Health.

McKillip, J. (1987). *Need analysis: Tools for the human services and education. Vol. 10: Applied Social Research Methods Series*. Newbury Park, CA: Sage Publications.

Needs Assessment Task Group. (1983). *The mental health needs assessment puzzle: A guide to a planful approach*. Columbus, OH: Ohio Department of Mental Health.

Panzarine, S. (1988). Teen mothering: Behaviors and intervention. *Journal of Adolescent Health Care, 9*, 443-448.

Rossi, P. H., Freeman, H. E., & Wright, S. R. (1979). *Evaluation: A systematic approach*. Beverly Hills, CA: Sage Publications.

Spearly, J. L., & Lauderdale, M. (1983). Community characteristics and ethnicity in the prediction of child maltreatment rates. *Child Abuse and Neglect, 7*, 91-105.

United Way. (1982). *Needs assessment: A guide for planners, managers, and funders of health and human care services*. Alexandria, VA: United Way.

Warheit, G. J., Bell, R. A., & Schwab, J. J. (1977). *Planning for change: Needs assessment approaches*. Washington, DC: National Institute for Mental Health.

# Designing a Child Abuse Prevention Project

A sound program design is the foundation of a successful program proposal. Through a decisionmaking process based on the needs assessment results and input from those connected with the program, a community need is joined to a solution.

The first step in designing a prevention project is to form a project planning group. This group meets to define the broad project goals and objectives with consideration given to realistic resource limitations. Through group discussion and decisionmaking, the project planning group writes a description of the project design that defines the problem the project addresses, including a description of the target population, and the solution(s) the program proposes.

The project planners must remain sensitive to a number of issues and factors throughout the planning process. Sometimes delicate political or community issues must be considered. In many cases, project planners deal with target populations that have cultural viewpoints and attitudes towards parenting different than their own. The needs assessment will provide most of the information required for dealing with these issues or factors. Additional input from representatives of the target population may also be valuable at this stage to let the target population know that they are partners in the project.

# Factors That Influence the Effectiveness of Prevention Programs

A major part of the designing process involves keeping in focus the primary factors that lead to an effective prevention program. Based on information gathered from a variety of human service prevention programs, Mueller and Higgins [1988] identified a number of factors that contribute to program effectiveness:

★ Correct identification and participation of an at-risk population

★ The ability to reach the at-risk population with the program

★ Appropriate timing of the prevention intervention

★ The use of (experiential) learning techniques in educational programs

★ Parental involvement in programs focusing on children or adolescents

★ Collaboration with other community services (e.g., networking and coordination with other community groups and programs)

★ Avoiding negative effects of prevention programs (e.g., arousing unnecessary fear in children)

# The Project Design Process

## Forming a Planning Team

The composition of the planning team can vary, but may include representatives from the project staff, key informants, the target population, and any others who may be involved in the implementation of the project (e.g., agency administrators, volunteers, etc.). Depending on the scope of the project, the group could be quite small, two to five members, but usually no more than eight to 12 members, or the planning process becomes unwieldy.

## The Planning Team's Responsibilities

The planning team outlines the organizational elements of the project with consideration given to the following:

★ The focus of the original project idea

★ The results obtained from the needs assessment

★ Gauging political climate and legal issues and keeping the design within the limits of government procedures and regulations

★ The costs and benefits of the proposed program

★ Possible duplication of services or competition from another provider

★ Input from project staff

★ Funder's requests and positions

★ Cultural differences and necessary policies and training to deal competently with these issues

## The Planning Meeting

There are several methods for beginning the project design. The **multi-meeting method** calls for the planning team to meet briefly and accept assignments for gathering or preparing various materials or information. Several short meetings from one to three hours can be scheduled, with each meeting accomplishing the design of some portion of the project. The **single meeting method** is an alternative method, which calls for the planning team to hold one intensive planning meeting, with the objective of completing the entire project design at one time.

Choose a method based on the following factors:

★ The number of persons and/or agencies involved in the project design and their schedules

★ The available resources and the time factor

★ The proposed scope of the project

★ Whether the funding source is known or must be found

★ The amount of information available from agencies, needs assessments, or other sources

Either choice of planning method requires that some or most of the preparations listed below be completed in order to produce a project design. These preparations will promote a productive meeting. Adjust them to fit the planning method selected.

## Meeting Preparations

★ Make a list of objectives for the meeting(s). (See "Program Goals and Objectives" on page 69 for more information on writing objectives.)

★ Develop an agenda(s) that covers all necessary decisionmaking aspects of the project design.

★ Select a person to lead the meeting(s) who understands the objectives, will adhere to the agenda, and who has experience working with groups.

★ Select a person to write the minutes accurately.

★ Bring key data to the meeting:

- Needs assessment results and analysis

- News releases or supporting data on needs, etc.

- A report on any history or resources of the sponsoring agency or resources offered by other sources

- Records or data supporting project budget proposal costs

- Proposed organizational structure, assignments, responsibilities, etc., that emerged from other preliminary discussions or meetings

- Other agency documentation, when applicable, such as a treasurer's report

- Funder's guidelines (see Chapter 5)

## *The Meeting Agenda(s)*

The meeting agenda(s) should include the following activities:

★ Review/discuss the needs assessment results.

★ Prepare a short history and description of resources of the sponsoring organization as they relate to the proposed project.

★ Prepare a description of the existing community environment and services or other factors that impact the proposed project.

★ Write a Mission Statement that shows how the sponsoring organization is compatible with the planned project's goals and objectives.

**Note:** A *Mission Statement* is a broad and comprehensive description of goals. It should be one short paragraph (approximately 25-30 words). Think of it as a public relations statement that could be published in a newspaper so that anyone could understand what the project is and what it does.

★ Prepare a description of the target population. List the characteristics that distinguish the target population from the rest of the population.

★ Identify any strengths and weaknesses of the staff or parent organization in regard to the planned project (e.g., use prior client or participant service records, volunteer or other participation, staff performance or expertise, financial responsibility, legislative contacts, public or media contacts, etc.).

★ Decide on proposed goals and objectives for the project and a plan of action to make the project work. These should be written in measurable terms. Include objectives that are specific, time limited, and measurable. Develop several key objectives that can be combined or adjusted to fit different funding requirements.

★ Decide on project intervention strategies that are specific (step-by-step).

★ Identify what is to be evaluated (e.g., staff performance, participant behavior, etc.).

★ Assign responsibility to individuals for gathering information on budget, hiring, or other project elements.

★ Develop a preliminary budget for the project.

★ Develop a plan for finding funding.

★ Develop a list of potential sources for support letters. Assign responsibility to individuals for obtaining letters of support.

### Meeting Guidelines

★ Plan enough time to cover the agenda.

★ During the meeting, write results on a flip chart and make copies for everyone present. Decide whether the meeting discussion content should be confidential.

★ Make sure task assignments are understood and deadlines for completion are clear and feasible.

## What Should the Planning Meeting(s) Produce?

The primary goal of the planning meeting is to obtain consensus on project goals and develop a project design. Generally, one or two people will be responsible for producing the actual project proposal based upon the results of the meeting and other information that is collected. The proposal usually includes the following:

★ Proposal summary

★ Introduction

★ Statement of the assessed need

★ Program goals and objectives

★ Intervention to achieve goals and objectives

★ Evaluation methods and procedures

★ Project budget and management plan

★ Future extension of the program and funding

★ Letters of support

The following sections explain these elements in detail.

## Proposal Summary

A reader forms the first impression of a proposal from the summary. It provides a critical opportunity to attract further interest in the project proposal. Include just enough concise and specific information about the project to pique the reader's curiosity to find out more. Present the necessary facts in an easy-to-read style. The following case's proposal was restricted to 50 words by the funder. However, other funders may allow more words for more detail. In general, keep the summary to 200 words or less.

### Case #9: Writing a Proposal Summary

Proposal Summary for the **Family Co-op Respite Care**, Franklin County, Ohio: "Family Co-op Respite Care project will strengthen family functioning and decrease the likelihood of abuse/neglect of children with disabilities by training parents how to provide cooperative respite care and support. The project will identify, recruit and select up to 30 families with at least one primary caregiver participating."

## Proposal Introduction

In this section, the proposal writer gives the project an identity. This is the place to bring out connections with highly visible people or to mention successes that have established a reputation. Employ a number of references that build credibility and support. Emphasize expertise that directly relates to the project. The credibility conveyed in this section may be the most important factor in obtaining funding. Remember to remain brief and specific and avoid jargon. Be sure to include these types of information in the introduction:

★ Years of related service or experience

★ Numbers of participants or clients served

★ Recent areas of interest and involvement and current activities

★ Materials developed

★ Awards received for related work

★ Specialized skills, training, or background, including degrees

★ Recognition, news articles, or presentations at conferences, publications, etc.

★ Previous grants/projects or other community service

★ Staff qualifications and specialized or related expertise

★ Comments from credible sources or quotes from support letters

## Needs Statement

Having established the project identity and credibility, the needs statement concentrates on conveying *why* the project is needed. This is where the needs must be stated and described based on the information obtained through the needs assessment.

Do not assume that everyone knows about the need(s). Provide enough description for anyone to come away with a clear picture about what the project is addressing. Be sure to define the need(s) in compatible and narrow enough terms so that the project appears feasible. Avoid depictions of the need(s) that are overly gloomy or seem insurmountable. Instead, present a need, support its existence with evidence, and concentrate on building the impression that solutions are possible within a reasonable amount of time and with available resources. Also avoid these two common errors when you construct a needs statement:

★ Be careful not to state that the need(s) is a result of a lack of the service that the program is offering. For instance: A high rate of low birth weight babies cannot be attributed to the lack of a teen pregnancy program. There may be other contributing factors, such as smoking, lack of transportation to medical care, etc.

★ Avoid saying a program is needed simply because it does not exist. The need must be documented.

### Document the Need(s)

★ Use evidence from the needs assessment to support the statement of the need.

★ Use *key* statistics. Present enough evidence to make a good case. Comparative statistics, those that show how one community or group compares to another, quickly make a point. If necessary, put additional graphs, charts, or tables in an appendix.

★ Present evidence from more than one source. Include qualitative evidence (e.g., authoritative statements from key informants), as well as quantitative evidence (comparative statistics).

★ Be careful to present data or evidence that really support the needs statement and do not inadvertently undermine the proposal. (Example: Do not use statistics that show a need in one community through comparison with another community where there is an even greater need for the service.)

See Cases #10 and #11 for examples of program narratives.

## Case #10: Writing a Statement of Needs

The **Family Co-op Respite Care** project worked with families who have children with disabilities. The program placed an emphasis on minority parents and single parents. Family functioning was strengthened through training parents how to provide cooperative respite care and support to each other.

The statement of need is based on research evidence: "Many parents experience at least occasional stressful forces that affect their abilities to function as part of healthy, nurturing, cohesive families. For parents of children with disabilities, these forces can become so strong, or go unrelieved so long, that crisis situations occur, and sometimes reoccur, frequently."

To support this statement of need, the narrative presents references to extensive research studies to establish the increased stresses and greater risk of maltreatment for such families and introduces the "solution": respite care.

"There are two major barriers for families of children with disabilities trying to secure respite care and support: 1) there aren't enough independently identified, competent caregivers, and 2) there are insufficient funds for public or private agencies to meet the needs .... It is also true that most families prefer in-home care by other family members, neighbors or friends ..."

These statements are supported by references to articles and several studies. In addition, the narrative states study findings that, "... of the range of services provided to families of children in out-of-home care, only 3.9% received respite care." The extremely limited funding and restrictive eligibility requirements of state programs are cited as another reason for an alternative program of respite care.

## Case #11: Writing a Statement of Needs

The **Parent Child Education Minority Project**, in Stark County, Ohio, reduces maltreatment by focusing on increasing parenting skill and reducing stress and isolation for minority parents. The project offers summer programs, outreach, and home visits. Other supports offered are literary skills, job readiness skills, and family counseling.

The statement of need is based on statistical evidence: The project builds a case for increasing the scope of the project through the use of statistics that show a large number of parents and children in the community fall into high-risk groups. The following statistics cover a wide range of characteristics that are frequently associated with being "at-risk," and the following statements are but a representative few used in the need statement:

- "Forty percent of all low birth weight babies came from Canton City (in Stark Co.) ... 56% of white births were under 3,500 grams and less, and 75.1% of black births were under 3,500 grams and less."

- "3,200 reported cases of abuse and neglect represent an increase of 400...44% of reported cases ... involve children 5 years and under ... Of 6,268 persons involved in reports, 2,000 were black—an increase of 400 last year."

- "Minority population of Stark County is 8% but reflects 14% of the Crisis Center caseload."

In addition to those statistics, other research report findings are used to show that "thirty-eight percent of the families in Canton City Schools are single-family households and the poverty level is higher (31%) than that of Stark County as a whole (13%)."

## Program Goals and Objectives

A project goal cites the result that the project wants to achieve. Since a single project is not likely to be aimed at eliminating all child maltreatment, the goal should be stated in relation to the scope of the project. It is here that you need to be specific about the type of abuse to be prevented and provide a working definition of that type of maltreatment.

To reach the goal, a project proposes a means of achieving this reduction of maltreatment. The means are called *objectives*.

★ A *goal* is a statement of the desired results that are wanted, such as changes in information, opinions, attitudes, and/or behaviors. These changes are referred to as *outcomes* and are achieved through the successful completion of specific measurable objectives.

★ An *objective* is a statement of the means of achieving a specific measurable program outcome that relates to the goal.

## *Developing Goals and Objectives*

Any prevention project must begin with operational goals and objectives. These are concrete statements of *what* the project is going to do and *how* it is going to do it. At first, it may be helpful to have the planning group frame these as questions. Have the project planners brainstorm a list of questions, broad and specific, that will need to be answered during the planning process. Listed below are examples of possible questions relating to the *target population*:

★ What are the characteristics and cultural or ethnic issues to be considered?

★ How will the participants be selected?

★ How many participants can be served?

★ What skills will the target population have to acquire or master in order to achieve the desired results?

Listed below are examples of possible questions relating to the *project*:

★ What type of maltreatment is being targeted?

★ What are the time frame, resource needs, and budget for the project?

★ How many staff persons will be needed to serve the population?

★ Where is the service location? What is the physical or geographic setting and circumstances that may influence participation?

★ How will the services be delivered (e.g., methods)?

★ How will the services be recorded or measured?

★ What are the existing legalities, jurisdictions, and protocols?

★ What other agencies or groups within the community can help or provide resources?

The planning group discusses this large list of questions so that they can make key decisions and reach consensus on the *goals* for the project.

Each project will have a unique design based on the particular goals and objectives of that project.

The next step is to develop clear statements for the goal(s) and objectives.

### Goal Statements

Goal statements should specifically relate to the identified problem and be realistic in terms of what can be achieved given the availability of resources and professional expertise. Following are some examples of goal statements taken from several projects funded by the Ohio Children's Trust Fund.

**Amish Parents Preventing Abuse:** "To develop a primary prevention parent education curriculum, and an outreach program to implement it, to protect children in the Amish community from child sexual abuse."

**Project HELP:** "To decrease the likelihood of physical abuse among children with special needs within the Columbus Public School system, through parent education workshops."

### Objective Statements

Objectives are the road maps that specify how a project will reach its goal. It is important to state objectives in measurable terms, otherwise there is no real way of knowing whether the objective is accomplished.

Objectives should have a relationship to the project goal. Avoid directing project time and resources toward achieving objectives that may be worthy, but do not support the specific project goal. To establish whether wanted changes occur, it is extremely important to develop objectives that contain the following elements.

★ Use action verbs rather than conceptual terms. A good rule to follow in writing objectives is to begin the objective with an action verb (e.g., identify, explain, revise, present, etc.).

★ Use measurable terms, so that when the proposal is written, each objective can be accompanied by the measurement method that will be used during the project. (See Cases #13 and #14 for examples of an objective accompanied by an evaluation method.)

★ Support and remain within the limitations of the project goal.

Following are some examples of objective statements taken from the projects cited above.

**Amish Parents Preventing Abuse:** "To select and convene a Community Steering Committee that will (a) act as an advocate for the program to the community, (b) guide the development of the parent education curriculum, and (c) develop the plan for implementing the curriculum."

**Project HELP:** "Plan 10 parent education workshops, two per community of school districts, for 200 parents."

Writing clear and achievable goals and objectives is a skill that is critical for obtaining funding for a project. See **Tool #5, Developing Objectives and Clear Statements of Need**, for more information on goals and objectives and writing recommendations.

## Intervention Methods to Achieve Goals and Objectives

This section of the design describes the methods that the project will use as solutions to the problem. Remember that simply stating these methods does not satisfy the reviewer as to why these methods were selected or why they would work. You must supply evidence that the methods were carefully and knowledgeably selected.

★ **Identify the observed attitudes, knowledge area, or behaviors to be affected by the program and why those methods should produce favorable results.** See Table 5 for examples of observable phenomena.

★ **Demonstrate cultural competence.** For instance, the method is suited to the cultural norms of a particular population, such as working through the elders within the Amish community, or an

**Table 5. Examples of Observable Phenomena**
- Parent hits child or uses time-out
- Parent knowledge of developmental milestones
- Parent praises child or parent belittles child
- Child arrives at school fed or dressed poorly or child arrives well-fed and appropriately dressed
- Parent attitude regarding corporal punishment

agency has an extensive history of success using a particular method with the target population.

★ **Give examples of results** obtained by other projects using these methods, or show how the methods had positive results in a similar circumstance and should have transferable success.

★ **Use research evidence that supports the program method**. Add "expert" testimony in support of the method selected.

In selecting program methods, be sure to consider several alternatives:

★ Make a list of the needs being addressed, the objectives, the possible methods of alleviating the needs, and the evaluation techniques that can be applied.

★ Use information about various interventions and strategies that other projects have used successfully.

- Consider the suggestions of the target population in adapting methods.

- Use the information from the needs assessment to adapt the intervention methods to suit the circumstances and the target population.

★ Have the project planners brainstorm the best possible solutions and alternatives. Case #12 illustrates an example of using supporting evidence for project methods.

## Case #12: Using Supporting Evidence for Project Methods

The **Comprehensive Advocacy For Minority Parents** (CAMP) project, Jefferson County, Ohio, was a multifaceted program of services, support, and training for minority teen parents and other single, at-risk parents. The project utilizes all appropriate local services to meet the needs of the target population through the use of advocates.

The CAMP project based its program on the success of two different projects, which the parent agency, Jefferson County Community Action Council, Inc., developed in working with high-risk parents who were not teenagers.

**Evidence of need:** "According to the nurse in charge of the maternity clinic at the Ohio Valley Hospital, where the public assistance clients are served, approximately 50% of the total case load are minority. However, among the young patients, about 75% are minority ... The minority population of Jefferson County is only 5.5% ... 21% of the single female caretakers receiving ADC are black .... We have found that young black clients more quickly develop a sense of trust when working with a black advocate because there is no perceived cultural gap ... Through our Consortium of Administrators from all the leading youth-serving agencies and through our Case Management Team of direct service professionals, we have not only identified the other agencies in the community and their relationship to the problem, but we have established an effective coordinated approach to providing services (members of the Consortium represent a broad range of services) ... we have developed a close relationship with the maternity unit at the local hospital..."

**Goal** (overall goal for several objectives): "To reduce the potential of child abuse and neglect through a comprehensive program of services for minority teen parents, as well as other single, at-risk minority parents."

**Objective** (one of four objectives): "To provide complete advocacy services for 10 new minority clients who are pregnant or parenting teens so that they will receive the appropriate health and social services."

### Intervention Methods

- Advocate makes home visits.

- Advocate makes hospital visits.

- Advocate provides emergency transportation.

- Advocate assists in providing basic resources.

## Evaluation

It is extremely important for project planners to include the selection and planning of evaluation procedures as a part of the initial program planning stage. It is quite difficult to add on an evaluation to a program already in progress. Therefore, it is advisable to plan program evaluation to correspond with each objective in the project design.

Maintaining objectivity is of primary consideration in planning for program evaluation. If possible, it is advisable to have the program evaluated by an outside agent. When this is not feasible, as is frequently the case, objective measurement procedures and instruments should be selected. See Chapter 7, "Project Evaluation," for more information about measurement instruments and evaluation procedures.

Case #13 and #14 show examples of project objectives and the evaluation methods selected by two project to measure achievement.

### Case #13: Selecting Objectives and Evaluation Methods

The **Parent Child Education Minority Project**, Stark County, Ohio, focused on engaging a higher percentage of minority families as participants in the existing parent education project.

**Program Objective:** "To provide center-based programming (i.e., parent education) at neighborhood centers to 150 parents."

**Evaluation Method:** "Pre- and postevaluation using the Family Assessment Device and Parent Participation Survey to measure parent participation, reduction in the incidence of inappropriate parenting techniques, and increased demonstration of knowledge of child development."

### Case #14: Selecting Objectives and Evaluation Methods

The **Take a Break Project**, a primary prevention initiative based in Jefferson, Ohio, provided positive parenting education materials to parents throughout Ohio by promoting the concept of "taking a break with your kids" as a part of family life. The Take a Break cards are distributed through fast food restaurants and contain information on parenting and family activities.

**Program Objective:** "To coordinate the development/revision, printing, production, and distribution of a series of parent education cards, with three new cards to be developed, and 1 million cards to be distributed."

**Evaluation Method:** "Maintain records of the number of cards printed and distributed and the location of distribution sites. Keep copies of media releases and gather copies of articles/columns/newsletters that result from the project."

## Budget and Management Plan

At the planning stage, a basic budget is all that is required. Realistically adapting the program objectives to the budget limitations enables the project to take on a look of feasibility. Basic management concerns and issues should be considered as part of the planning process in anticipation of such implementation factors as time, expense, and scheduling. (Refer to Chapters 5 and 6 for more detailed information on budget and management.) A skeleton budget includes the following:

★ Personnel costs (wages, benefits, consultant costs)

★ Nonpersonnel costs:

- Equipment rental, lease, or purchase

- Project materials (booklets, charts, etc.)

- Consumable supplies (office supplies, food/beverages, etc.)

- Travel

- Telephones

- Miscellaneous (postage, insurance, subscriptions, publications, printing costs, etc.)

- Indirect costs (rent, utilities, bookkeeping, payroll, maintenance, etc.)

- Participant incentives or costs for transportation, child care, etc.

- In-kind contribution (any project cost donated by the sponsoring agency or other organization)

Basic management procedures should include the following:

★ Licensing requirements and forms

★ Staff requirements and selection process, job descriptions, training procedures

★ Policies (reporting or other office procedures)

★ Staff responsibility assignments and chain of command

★ Recruitment and training of volunteers

★ Reports and documentation of the project

## Future Funding

Funding resources are limited, and there is growing competition for them. Funders often require a plan for program continuation and future funding. Sometimes programs can be transitioned to fee-for-service or become part of an agency's operational budget. In other cases, outside funding will continue to be required. In any case, explain and justify your plans for the future. (Chapter 5 covers project funding in more detail.)

## Letters of Support

Letters of support are professional references confirming a project's viability and the competence of the project's staff to successfully implement the project. Also, other agencies or organizations can recount past instances of successful collaboration and ways and means of offering assistance or support to the proposed project. Ask for letters of support from prominent individuals who are community "gatekeepers," as well as from the directors of collaborating agencies. Letters of support should contain the following elements, when applicable:

★ Brief descriptions of past collaboration

★ Observations regarding the sponsoring agency for the project and/ or project staff's qualifications

★ Statement(s) regarding the need for the project, which show its specific worth to the community

★ Statement(s) indicating willingness to collaborate or a commitment of staff time, use of equipment, donations, etc.

## Finalizing the Project Design and Finding Funding

Once the proposal is drafted, it is advisable to have all members of the planning group review it and offer suggestions, as well as finalize their support for the project. The groundwork for the prevention project is now complete, and a proposal based on the agreed-upon design can be submitted to prospective funders. The next chapter, "Project Funding," will cover the steps in preparing for formal application for funding.

## References

Conners, T. D. (Ed.). (1980). *The nonprofit organization handbook*. New York: McGraw-Hill.

Elkin, R., & Vorwailer, D. J. (1972, May). Evaluating the effectiveness of social services. *Management Controls* (Peat, Marwick, Mitchell and Company), pp. 104-111.

Kiritz, N. J. (1980). *Program planning & proposal writing: Expanded version*. Reprinted from *The Grantsmanship Center News* as part of The Grantsmanship Center Reprint Series on Program Planning & Proposal Writing. Available from The Grantsmanship Center, 1031 S. Grand Avenue, Los Angeles, CA 90015.

Mueller, D. P., & Higgins, P. S. (1988). *Funders' guide manual: A guide to prevention programs in human services: Focus on children and adolescents*. St. Paul, MN: Amherst H. Wilder Foundation. Available from Community Care Resources, Amherst H. Wilder Foundation, 919 Lafond Avenue, St. Paul, MN 55104.

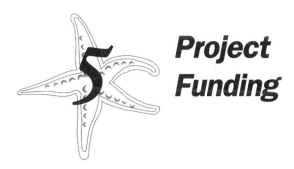

# Project Funding

**In this chapter ...**

Gather a broad base of information about funding sources:

★ Cultivate and use professional and community contacts as a network

★ Use specialized resource centers, funding publications, and libraries

★ Learn about the different sources and types of funding

★ Learn about the funding process and work with it

Submit proposals that are based on sound research about the funder:

★ Learn about the potential funder's areas of emphasis and bias

★ Follow the guidelines for writing and submitting a proposal

A well-designed project can optimistically direct its energy toward obtaining funding. The critical preparation work was accomplished by the needs assessment and project design process, and the project is now ready to seek funding. The project funding strategy builds on the following strengths:

The **needs assessment results** established a well-documented need or gap in community services.

**Contact with key informants** in the assessment and design stages established valuable community support, as well as a network to locate and obtain funding.

The **design reflects input from a variety of sources** contributing to a proposed program that has carefully matched interventions to needs and built in necessary cultural awareness.

# Finding Funding Sources

Gathering a broad base of information about possible funding sources is the beginning step in locating a sponsor for the project. Listed below are some recommended sources.

★ **Use the Internet.** Many large foundations, as well as government agencies, have websites with funding information and even application forms. See Appendix B for a listing of the federal sources of funding for child abuse prevention activities.

★ **Establish a network of contacts** in the community, including professionals, political figures, corporate executives, and others who may know of funding sources and may even have personal contacts on foundation boards or at public funding sources. (It's usually helpful to have some preliminary contact with the potential funder, and having a personal contact greatly facilitates this process and is likely to increase the amount of informal advice that the funder may give you.)

★ **Research local foundations** that will fund child abuse prevention. Build a relationship with them before you apply for a grant. Invite them to site visits at your agency or program. Generally, they are more accessible and less competitive than national organizations, since most only fund local programs.

★ **The Foundation Center** is an extremely useful source of information about foundations. It is a nonprofit organization that not only collects information about foundations, but also provides analysis of the information and makes it available through publications and services. It has an extensive library. See Table 6 for more information about The Foundation Center.

★ **A less common source of funding is through a negotiated contract** with a local or state private or public agency to provide such services as training or technical assistance in the area of prevention.

### Table 6. The Foundation Center

1-800-424-9836 • http://www.fdncenter.org

<u>National Collections</u>

79 Fifth Avenue New York, NY 10003; 212/620-4230

1001 Connecticut Avenue NW, Suite 938, Washington, DC 20036
202/331-1400;

<u>Field Offices</u>

312 Sutter Street, San Francisco, CA 94108; 415/397-0902

1356 E. 14th Street, Cleveland, OH 44115; 216/861-1933

The following information is also available from the Foundation Center (cost involved in some instances):

★ Foundation IRS filings (990-PF Forms) and annual reports on microfiche (e.g., fiscal data, addresses, telephone numbers, officers, and grants lists).

★ *The Foundation Directory* contains factual information and is found in many libraries.

★ *The Foundation Grants Index* has a current subject index on recent grants as part of the bimonthly periodical, *Foundation News*. The index helps identify funder interest or subject areas previously funded as well as the geographical location of different foundations.

★ *About Foundations* is a reasonably priced guide especially geared to help projects looking for funding by offering decisionmaking information.

★ *Source Book Profiles* contains information about foundations: program interest, financial information, names of people to contact or know about and particular foundation specifics like recent grants, application dates, and guidelines.

★ *The Foundation Center National Data Book* lists active private foundations and shows if a report is published.

In addition, the Foundation Center offers these services:

★ Special orientations regarding the use of materials

★ Publications for sale

★ Special topics information, especially on nonprofit management

★ Check the *Federal Register* sections, "Notices for Discretionary Funds Program and Availability of Funds and Request for Applications."

★ Request to be put on the mailing lists of potential funding sources that periodically put out RFPs (e.g., state agencies, Children's Trust Funds).

★ Subscribe to newsletters that alert readers to potential funding sources. (See Appendix E for listings.)

## What Are the Major Funding Sources?

Funding comes from two sources: government funds (federal, state, or local) or private funds (foundations, bequests, private donations, and corporate support).

All funding sources have some special interest that they are either mandated to serve or elect to serve. Because of this specialized focus, a project proposal must show how and why it meets the criteria of the funder. The closer the proposal can come to matching the interests of the funder, the more likely a project will receive a favorable review and receive funding.

Using the right terminology can be important. For example, a funder may have an interest in "family support programs," rather than child abuse prevention per se. Writing the proposal using that term may greatly enhance the chances of getting funded without appreciably altering the goals or objectives of the program. Child abuse prevention, in reality, does go by different names—choose the one that the funder uses.

Many funding sources welcome the opportunity to collaborate on developing a prevention idea.

★ **Federal, state, and local funds** are generally tied through legislation to specific areas of need with some money allocated for discretionary purposes. Traditionally, government funding has had to show a connection to the public welfare. Also, funding decisions are sometimes based on cost and effectiveness as related to numbers of persons served. However, there are grants awarded to new or innovative pilot projects as seed money as well as to projects viewed as serving special needs.

Most states have some form of Children's Trust Fund specifically dedicated to funding child abuse prevention activities. The program focus, dollars available, and application procedures are specific to each state fund.

CONTACT INFORMATION: For current information about your state's fund, go to the website of the National Alliance of Children's Trust and Prevention Funds at *http://pilot.msu.edu/user/millsda/index.html*.

★ **Corporate** giving is often dependent on serving the corporate "image." Corporations are willing to serve the public welfare but are most willing to do so in ways that also enhance corporate success as well.

★ **Foundations** also address social action issues, but can narrowly define specific areas of interest based upon donors' and/or board members' interests. The following section discusses foundations in more detail.

## *Foundations*

There are many kinds of foundations. Many are small and interested in serving local populations by funding local projects. Therefore, it is advantageous to do some homework on foundations to find out about how they operate and their patterns of funding before spending time and energy on preparing and submitting a project proposal.

The following types of foundations are the most likely to be a source of funding for a prevention project. These foundations fall into two categories in their funding patterns: either funding for a specific purpose or funding for a number of general purposes.

★ **Corporate foundations** use money donated by the company. Generally, the grants go to programs that benefit the company in some way—either by serving employees of the company, serving the area in which the company is located, or serving as a public relations tool.

★ **Community foundations** operate using donations from community businesses, or private trusts, or bequests. As a rule, they serve community-based programs. These foundations make frequent public reports, so they are easy to identify and profile. Some are quite large (e.g., the Cleveland Foundation), while others are limited in scope.

★ **Family foundations** are used by private individuals as a means of directing their donations towards specific areas of interest. Contact is often made through the family's office, law firm, or bank. Larger foundations may have a professional staff.

Many foundations prefer mail communication, and some do not have publicly listed telephone numbers. Find the address and contact person in *The Foundation Directory* or in the Foundation Center's *National Data Book*. (See Table 6, The Foundation Center.)

Sometimes it is possible to "piece together" funding from several sources to cover the entire project cost. Obtaining one grant, even a small one, enhances project credibility and provides leverage for obtaining additional funds from other sources.

## Preparing to Submit a Proposal

Preparation of a grant proposal requires an investment of time and energy. Therefore, carefully select one or more appropriate funders before making an application for funding. Choose funders with a frame of reference and interests that are compatible with the project's goals and objectives. For example, is there a bias toward a specific type of program or for serving a specific population?

Every funder will have specific application guidelines that must be followed. Sometimes funders require a preliminary application procedure. For instance, some government agencies and many foundations request a two- or three-page prospectus or concept paper as an initial proposal. If there is interest in the concept paper, the funder will request a full proposal. In this case, be sure to include the most essential components of the proposal and leave out additional explanatory information.

In approaching any potential funding source, it is beneficial to adapt the following recommendations.

★ **Become informed about the funding source.** Find out as much as possible about the funder from other sources and from the funder. Relevant information includes the following:

- Geographical funding area

- Range of funding amounts

- Types of projects supported in the past

- Traditional or innovative preferences

- Funding periods, application deadlines

- Project compatibility with funder's image, previous funding record, and current interests and priorities

- Amount of competition for funder's money

- Compatibility of project's design and funder's criteria

★ **Communicate carefully with a potential funder.**

- Leave a good impression with every contact made with the funder.

- Communicate a willingness to work with the funder. Some changes may have to be made to the project. However, do not destroy the integrity of the project if a funder requests too many changes. Instead, try to find another funder with more compatible interests.

★ **Follow the funder's directions** precisely when submitting a proposal.

- Comply with deadlines, proposal format requirements, or preferences or other special features (e.g., letters of recommendation or support, specific numbers of objectives, word number limitations, etc.).

★ **Write the proposal with some knowledge of the funder's perspective.** The *Funder's Guide Manual* [Mueller & Higgins 1988] presents a number of key areas that funders cover when reviewing a project proposal:

- Extent of the estimated program impact on the need

- Evidence that the program will identify and reach the target population

- Prevention-focused program activities

- Potential effectiveness of the program, based on a sound model that reflects current knowledge

- Consistency between the type and duration of the intervention and the level of risk of the population

- Introduction of program interventions at the most opportune time to be effective

- Minimized risks to the program participants

- Evidence of coordination between the program and existing community services

- Adequate community acceptance and support for the program

- Cost compares positively to other programs

- An evaluation component sufficient to measure the outcome

★ **Attend technical workshops** that a funder may offer, which are specifically geared for making proposals. Generally, these are only offered by government agencies.

★ **Obtain appropriate support letters** and letters of promise or cooperation (e.g., referrals from another agency are confirmed by the agency in writing).

## Submitting a Proposal

Whenever possible, obtain detailed directions from the funder about the content and format of a proposal. **Follow these exactly**. When detailed directions are not forthcoming, use the following guidelines in preparing a proposal.

### Cover Letter

★ Refer to the most recent conversation or meeting.

★ Put in a *brief* description of the content of the proposal.

★ If appropriate, volunteer to meet with the funder or make a presentation.

★ Close with a carefully worded, optimistic statement.

### Proposal Format

★ Title page with short, clear title.

★ Table of contents consistent with proposal headings.

★ Number all pages the same way (except the first page). Use standard-sized paper (8" x 11").

★ Staple pages, upper left corner (do not use elaborate covers, plastic page covers, etc.). Do not fold or bend the proposal.

★ Make page breaks between sections whenever possible

### Proposal Style

★ Present the proposal using clear, concise statements. Avoid jargon and put yourself in the place of the reader who may know little about this topic. A balanced presentation containing forceful statements of needs and solutions followed with adequate and accurate documentation is best.

## Proposal Content

★ Abstract or summary

★ Description of the agency or project group making the proposal

★ Statement of need(s)

★ Goals and objectives

★ Methods/interventions to meet need(s)

★ Evaluation methods

★ Organizational and management description:

- Staff job descriptions

- Organization and responsibility assignment

- Timeline

- Facilities

- Budget figures and narrative

- Continuation of the project

★ Future funding

★ Appendices and attachments

★ Support letters

## Budget

Most funders specify a number of budget categories or "line items." A proposal will generally not be turned down simply because of the budget request. The funder, however, may request a revised budget or agree to fund only one portion of the entire program. Use the budget narrative to justify program expenses, explain any unusual items, and generally demonstrate fiscal responsibility. Be precise in explaining expenses: e.g., 30 parent education pamphlets @ $3.00/participant. Remember to aim for consistency between budget items and proposal description.

★ **Direct costs (costs directly funded for the project)**

- Personnel

- Consultants

- Travel

- Supplies (office, other)

- Telephone/utilities/postage

- Equipment rental or purchase

- Copying/printing

- Project materials/supplies

- Miscellaneous (anything that does not fit other categories)

★ **Indirect costs (funds requested for "overhead")**

- Office space/equipment/support staff time for bookkeeping or payroll, administrative overhead, etc.

★ **In-kind contributions**

- Any of the items listed above that the project or agency donates to the project budget (administrative time, office space, etc.)

The total project cost is the sum of direct costs, indirect costs, and in-kind contributions.

It is important to be aware of all the "details" specified by the funder and adjust the proposal to accommodate them. Give adequate attention to the following:

★ Restrictions in use of funds (e.g., cannot purchase equipment)

★ Approval or restrictions on travel in/out of state

★ Ownership of equipment or materials purchased with funded money

★ The "matching" requirements (e.g., money, items, or time donated from another source)

## What Do Experienced Prevention Projects Say About Finding Funding?

Professionals representing 20 Ohio Children's Trust Fund prevention projects volunteered the following advice.

### *Groundwork for Funding*

★ Begin with a good assessment of community needs.

★ Review the literature to find documentation and to find project intervention ideas that have proven successful.

★ Compile factual evidence from research and statistics to support the project proposal.

★ Make use of key informants, gatekeepers, and other influential contacts from all areas of the community and in all levels of government and network with them to suggest possible funding sources.

★ Advocate for prevention by increasing the individual awareness of influential persons, as well as general community awareness. Make use of available media to heighten public awareness of the effectiveness of prevention. Use talk shows, public forums, and speaking opportunities to generate support and allies.

★ Capitalize on human interest events that bring maltreatment issues into public focus. Use them as part of the statement of need.

★ Show how business interests can enhance their public image from promoting and supporting prevention efforts. Use marketing techniques, presentations, etc.

★ Work with schools or other parent/child groups to educate and convince the community about the value of prevention programs.

★ Communicate with other agencies and find out what they do. Attend health fairs, school open houses, fundraisers.

★ Approach the most powerful media personalities in the community and cultivate their support as verbal sponsors.

### Submitting Proposals

★ Locate several possible funding sources and apply to them one at a time.

★ Carefully follow funder directions in writing the proposal.

★ Communicate with the funder to gain more in-depth explanations and directions about what the funder wants.

★ Continuously gather information about future funding areas.

★ Contact fund-raising professionals to gain assistance or write the grant (if allowed).

★ Use samples of successful grant applications as models.

★ If rejected initially, resubmit the grant. Try to get feedback from the funder, make changes, and try again.

## Avoid the Major Mistakes That Lead to Proposal Rejection

The results of several studies that looked at why proposals are rejected have turned up four major mistakes to avoid in writing a project proposal [Krathwohl 1977]:

★ The problem or "need" addressed by the project:

- Not considered significant enough to warrant funding

- Not clearly stated

- Depicted as too great to be adequately addressed by the project

- Insufficiently supported by research or other evidence

★ The procedure or "method(s)" of addressing the need:

- Poorly described and lacked enough description and detail

- Poorly matched with stated objective

- Inadequate to properly select participants or to deal with barriers to service delivery

- Unable to be adequately evaluated using described procedures

★ The personnel to implement the project:

- Were inadequately trained or experienced and no explanation was provided to compensate for this (e.g., training, use of consultants, etc.)

- Were insufficiently described (e.g., qualifications, availability, etc.)

★ Inadequacies in other areas of the proposal:

- The cost of the project (budget) was deemed to be too high for expected results, and/or

- The funder was asked to assume costs that should belong to the parent agency

These studies also found that well-prepared projects designed to meet well-assessed needs submit more favorable proposals than projects designed primarily to obtain funding that is available.

## Make Final Revisions

Before submitting the proposal, it is advisable to have one or more qualified persons review it and make comments. Make any necessary changes or revisions and do a final check:

★ Is the format clean (e.g., spelling, punctuation, page numbers, etc., are checked)?

★ Does the proposal follow all the funder's guidelines and directions?

★ Are the goals, objectives, and evaluation methods clear and consistent with the stated need?

★ Are all the supporting materials, letters, or recommendations attached and necessary approvals and signatures in place?

The proposal is now ready to be submitted.

## The Proposal Review Process

Each foundation or funder will follow specific guidelines when receiving a proposal.

★ **Federal grant proposals** are reviewed by convening a panel of nationally recognized experts in the topic area. The panel follows a standard review process based on a point system, which is usually stated in the RFP. The federal officials use data from the panel of experts to award points to proposals and determine the recipient(s) of the grant.

★ **Foundations** follow individual processes and usually the foundation staff and/or board members are the reviewers.

★ **State Children's Trust Funds** follow individual procedures.

### What to Do When Funding Is Approved

Most project proposals receiving approval for funding are returned with requests for changes, adaptations, additions, and/or corrections. It is important to carefully consider how such changes will affect the integrity of the original proposal:

★ Will the impact of the project intervention be altered substantially?

★ Will the program be able to be adequately evaluated?

★ Will community support and contribution be affected?

★ Have other issues, such as the project's ability to demonstrate cultural awareness or to adequately train staff, been affected by the changes?

★ Is the amount of money granted adequate to implement the project?

★ Reassess the feasibility of implementing the project based on an evaluation of the preceding issues. This is especially critical if a long period of time passed between the application and the approval, because cost estimates or availability of staff may be affected.

## Accepting Funding

At this stage, open communication with the funder is critical. Discuss any reservations and questions regarding changes in the proposal or procedural issues. If certain changes are not acceptable, be sure to support objections with evidence as part of the explanation.

After negotiations are finished, confirm any changes with the funder. Accept funding only if it appears possible to implement the project successfully with the funded amount. If the changes are agreeable, write them into the proposal and resubmit it with a letter of acceptance. If there is substantial concern that the changes will alter the project's effectiveness, try to find another funder with more similar interests.

When final acceptance is received, notify everyone who participated in assessment and planning stages, as well as any others who will be a part of the project or have an interest in the project.

## Continued Funding

Maintaining funding for a program past the pilot stage has always posed the greatest challenge to successful projects. Just because a project is successful does not guarantee its continuation—a successful project requires the following for continued funding:

★ A sound evaluation

- Show success. Good evaluation procedures and methods are the best means of doing this.

★ Good public relations

- Communicate project success to a wide audience through the good use of community contacts and media.

- Cultivate contacts and involve community business leaders, agencies, and civic groups early in the project.

- Emphasize the unique aspects of the project (e.g., culturally aware, reaches a population that other projects or agencies have failed to reach, etc.).

★ A realistic plan for future funding

- Consider forming joint funding arrangements by combining corporate and community or agency support.

- Consider transitioning to a fee-for-service arrangement, fund-raising, or adding a fee-for-service component, (such as trainings) to the program.

## The Next Step: Implementation

Congratulations! Funding has been awarded to your project. The prevention idea is about to become a reality and the next step is to convert the design into a functioning project. This implementation phase builds upon the work done in assessment and designing stages and brings the project to life. The next chapter, "Implementing a Project," will cover information and issues related to getting the project started and operating the project.

## References

Conners, T. D. (Ed.). (1980). *The nonprofit organization handbook.* New York: McGraw-Hill.

Kiritz, N. J. (1980). *Program planning & proposal writing: Expanded version*. Reprinted from *The Grantsmanship Center News* as part of The Grantsmanship Center Reprint Series on Program Planning & Proposal Writing. Available from The Grantsmanship Center, 1031 S. Grand Avenue, Los Angeles, CA 90015.

Krathwohl, D. R. (1977). *How to prepare a research proposal: Suggestions for those seeking funds for behavioral science research* (2nd ed.). Available from the Syracuse University Bookstore, 303 University Place, Syracuse, New York, 13210.

Mueller, D. P., & Higgins, P. S. (1988). *Funder's guide manual: A guide to prevention programs in human services: Focus on children and adolescents*. St. Paul, MN: Amherst H. Wilder Foundation. Available from Community Care Resources, Amherst H. Wilder Foundation, 919 Lafond Avenue, St. Paul, MN, 55104.

U.S. Department of Health and Human Services, Office of Human Development Services. (1991, March 14). *Federal Register, 56* (50) (FR Doc. 91-5828).

# *Implementing a Project*

Once the prevention project idea has evolved into a concrete project design and you have obtained funding for the project, it is time for project implementation to begin. All the previous preparation work should make this stage of the project go relatively smoothly. Because a prevention program is people and service oriented, however, be prepared to adapt the program when necessary. (If you are considering significant changes, you should notify the funder.)

The first step in implementing a project is to establish the organizational plan. Review the project plan, the goal(s) and objectives, as well as the intervention methods. Make a timeline of project events to help bring the project into focus. Break up the details of implementation into categories, such as those presented in this chapter, and use them as guides to systematically achieve the project goals and objectives. It is also important to review all details of the project and make adjustments to correspond to any changes agreed upon with the funder as part of the final funding arrangement.

# The Organizational Framework

The organizational framework of the project combines management and operational plans to coordinate and set the guidelines for all of the project activities. Develop a visual plan in the form of a chart or timeline, along with descriptions of policies and procedures covering all stages and components of the implementation process. It is a good idea to keep all management and operational information organized in a file or notebook and make it easily accessible for staff. Explain all procedures and policies to each staff person individually or as part of a group orientation.

## The Management and Operational Plan

1. Set dates for interviewing, hiring, or contracting with staff or consultants, as well as for orientation session and training workshops.

2. Describe all vital project activities, the beginning and ending dates of the activities, and the person responsible for overseeing the accomplishment of each activity and reporting the results.

   ★ Set accomplishment dates for developing materials, recruiting volunteers, and recruiting participants.

   ★ Plan and coordinate dates for participant training or activity sessions.

   ★ Set specific dates for monitoring or reviewing project progress toward meeting goals and objectives.

   ★ Make arrangements with other agencies or organizations for referrals.

★ Plan public relations activities or dates to inform key community contacts about the project.

3. Coordinate documentation dates and procedures to fit project activities.

   ★ Set pre- and posttest administration due dates.

   ★ Schedule progress report due dates or meetings required by an agency or funder.

   ★ Schedule evaluation analysis due dates.

4. Plan and schedule other activities, such as special trainings or conferences to organize or attend.

5. Describe the chain of command and show who has responsibility for specific activities, as well as who each staff person is to report to or supervise.

   ★ Develop procedures for communicating recommendations or complaints.

   ★ Prepare employee job descriptions, benefits, etc.

6. Develop and describe policies and procedures.

   ★ Clearly describe the limits of participant/staff interactions.

   ★ Clearly describe the areas of confidentiality in a policy statement.

   ★ Develop a policy for reporting suspected maltreatment in accordance with legal requirements, as well as a procedure for making the policy known to participants. (See Appendix F.)

7. Prepare project "description" messages for public relations purposes.

## Project Personnel

Qualifications, experience, and attitude are of primary importance when selecting staff. Educational background, experience, interpersonal skills, familiarity with a specific culture, or other expertise should be weighed carefully in making staffing decisions. For example, a project that must have staff with the ability to work in a culturally aware manner with a particular population may give more weight to those qualifications and/ or skills than to professional credentials. It is also important to consider whether staff personalities will be compatible.

★ The project director or coordinator holds the most responsibility for successfully implementing a project. Therefore, it is critical to select a person with excellent qualifications and experience.

★ If current agency personnel will staff the project, carefully select and match staff expertise and experience with the project responsibilities.

★ Make sure staff are committed to the concept of nonviolent child rearing and are in agreement with the program philosophy and approach.

★ Recruit and select volunteers based on qualifications and experience, as well as their motivation for volunteering. Orient them so that they can become familiar with policies and procedures.

### Using Consultants

Some personnel needs can be dealt with effectively by using consultants. Evaluate the benefits of using a consultant as well as the consultant's expertise in relation to the project. The box on page 103 shows examples of positive and negative consequences experienced by projects using consultants.

### Using Volunteers

Many projects can benefit from using volunteers in a number of capacities (e.g., clerical, community liaison, artists, speakers, puppeteers, data entry, etc.). Some projects make use of volunteers as a means of establishing important ongoing contact with participants and the community.

## Using Consultants

Positive experience: **Project HELP**, Franklin County, Ohio, successfully used consultants from Head Start to provide feedback on the value of materials and project presentations that were incorporated into the second year of the project. A group of elementary school principals also served as consultants and suggested ideas for recruiting participants for a parent training session for parents of children with disabilities. Acting upon their advice, incentives (i.e., grocery store coupons) were used to attract participants. The principals recognized that parents, in many cases, would have to sacrifice pay to attend the trainings. The incentives offset this loss. The principals also became advocates for the program and helped with distribution of flyers.

Difficult experience: The **Cambodian Abuse Prevention Project**, Franklin County, Ohio, found that working with a consultant created difficulties, because the consultant, although a professional, was not culturally in tune with the project's population and made recommendations that were culturally inappropriate. The project staff spent a great deal of time explaining the cultural reasons why the recommendations were not appropriate and felt uncomfortable about disagreeing with an "expert." Eventually, it was found to be more helpful to interview and work with key informants within the target population (i.e., religious leaders), because they had more grassroots knowledge about the community and could offer culturally appropriate solutions.

The key to success: Find the consultant who has the right expertise and can work flexibly with project personnel and adjust to individual project needs. Contact people who have hired the consultant for their recommendations.

The use of volunteers may be the only way a project can feasibly be implemented, especially when working with limited funding. Volunteers frequently become the backbone of continuing community support for a project and advocate for abuse prevention, and they are often the greatest source of enthusiasm. See **Tool #6, Working with Volunteers**, for more information.

## The Location of the Project

The selection of a location or facility where program services will be provided or performed depends on the focus of the project. Many projects use space provided by a parent agency or made available by a community organization or business. In some cases, the needs assessment has shown that locating the program services within easy access of the target population is a primary consideration for successful service provision. More than one site may be needed to meet the needs of the target population.

### Selecting a Facility or Location for a Program

★ Check local schools, social service agencies, libraries, hospitals, colleges, churches, business or corporate facilities, or other community group facilities when looking for facilities. Ask about rental information, restrictions, and responsibilities.

  - Check the location for acceptability by the target population (e.g., using church facilities may deter participants of another faith).

★ Choose a location that is accessible to the target population; look along major bus routes or provide transportation.

★ Check the location for acceptability, etc. If the program is oriented towards training, education, social functions, or combinations of these, visit different locations and look for the following:

  - A large enough room for full attendance (picture people in the setting)

  - A room where materials can be easily displayed and are easily visible

  - A reasonably soundproof room, one that can be darkened for viewing slides or films and with an adjustable thermostat, sufficient outlets, good lighting, etc.

See Case #15 for an example of selecting a site.

### Case #15: Selecting a Program Site

The **Parenting Plus Project**, Cuyahoga County, Ohio, used recommendations from administrators at Head Start to identify Head Start locations that were most in need of the project's services and were also in areas that reflected a cross section of the population. For these activities, the facility had to be easily accessible by the parents as well as by the volunteer parent partners who were mainly senior citizens. The administrators suggested local sites in churches and community centers that suited the accessibility requirements of both the participants and the volunteers.

### *Setting the Time for Sessions, Meetings, or Events*

★ Check bus schedules for regular service times or confirm availability of other transportation (e.g., volunteers).

★ Check for other conflicting commitments or barriers that participants may experience (e.g., church or other group activities, school events, religious observances, child care, etc.).

★ Schedule the date and time with consideration of safety factors (e.g., after dark may not be a good time in certain neighborhoods).

## *Equipment and Office Materials*

Every project produces correspondence, makes copies, and uses telephones or other equipment and materials. Equipment and materials should be purchased, leased, or shared as specified in the grant. Some projects may need sophisticated equipment to develop state-of-the-art materials, while other projects may have only occasional need for secretarial, copying, or print services.

When using equipment or secretarial time, establish and adhere to access and usage schedules that are arranged with parent agencies or with community businesses that donate use of equipment or staff time. Make arrangements that correspond with project activity accomplishment dates and goals. Also, keep accurate logs or records of time usage and materials for budget purposes.

Excellent and affordable computer software to manage project operations, maintain records, analyze data, and develop attractive program materials has become available in the last few years. Sophisticated computer resources are now within the reach of every project. Using this software can improve program efficiency and keep costs down. Project staff, however, must be properly trained to use the software.

## Project Documentation

When a project accepts funding, it also accepts a responsibility to show accountability. Documentation of all project activities and expenditures makes this easy. Establish good documentation and filing procedures for project personnel to follow. Assign someone the responsibility of monitoring the files periodically to check on whether the files are current and accurate. Timely entry of information, thorough record keeping, and a good filing system enable a project to easily access facts and figures to use in progress reports and as evidence of program effectiveness.

### Establish a Filing System That Uses Logical Categories

Each project may have specialized files. The following list contains some of the most common file categories:

★ General correspondence and correspondence with the funder

★ Publicity information, such as articles, comments, letters of recommendation

★ Expenditures and donations received

★ Volunteer information

★ Release forms

★ Official documents/grant agreements/contracts

★ Personnel and volunteer files

★ Mailing lists of key informants or key contacts who should receive periodic updates about the project

### *Documentation of Project Activities and/or Performance*

Establish a procedure and method for making written comments or completing a checklist after every project activity, so that these entries can be used to suggest program changes or used later as part of the project evaluation. Follow a policy and procedure to provide a record of entries to demonstrate progress towards meeting project objectives. Note changes in behaviors or attitudes for project participants which occur as a result of intervention methods or to compare effects due to changes or adaptations in presentation, materials, or curriculum. More information on documentation of project performance is contained in Chapter 7, "Project Evaluation."

### *Financial Records*

Financial records should correspond to the funder's requirements for reporting. Set up a bookkeeping system that accurately tracks project expenditures, volunteer hours, indirect costs, and in-kind contributions. Many funders require an independent audit report of the sponsoring agency at the end of the fiscal year.

### *Forms and Releases*

There are any number of forms that a project uses for documentation purposes. Certain forms are necessary to restrict liability or as explanations of the project or project procedures and policies. There are many standardized forms that can be easily adapted for a particular use. Check with contacts at agencies or government departments for samples of forms. Adapt a similar format or content to suit the individual project's purposes.

If adapting or designing specialized forms, be sure the form is easily understood and uses simple language (layman's terms, if possible). Avoid terms that are not commonly known, but if this is unavoidable, provide definitions and examples. Keep forms short and ask for only the information needed for the project. Long, tedious forms discourage participants and result in incomplete or inaccurate information. Following are some suggestions for using forms:

★ Intake/information forms contain personal information such as address, phone, work numbers, physician numbers, as well as basic information about family members, medical history, etc. Use intake forms to collect information that can be used as baseline data and as a description of the target population.

★ It is extremely important to have staff complete forms that permit the release of information for background searches on prior criminal convictions or involvement in substantiated child maltreatment. (In some states, such as Ohio, this is required by state law for certain types of employment.) A project should protect itself by doing a background check on all staff or volunteers regarding perpetration of child maltreatment.

★ Forms should indicate when information is provided voluntarily and protected by rights and privacy legislation.

★ Forms should indicate whether any information or discussion is confidential, and all staff, including volunteers, should be informed of confidentiality restrictions.

★ Some projects may have equipment use forms, telephone or mail logs, etc., for scheduling or accounting purposes.

★ Progress report forms monitor changes in participants at each contact with a project.

★ Participants may benefit from existing community services, and a referral form can be a helpful way to initiate contact with another service provider.

Case #16 contains an example of a project that used a number of forms, releases, and information sheets throughout the course of the project.

### Case #16: Using Forms, Releases, and Information Sheets Effectively

The **Parenting Plus Project** taught parenting skills to Head Start parents and also provided social support to them through volunteers called "parent partners." The project used a variety of forms:

Participant/Personnel

Parent Consent to Participate Form

Volunteer Agreement to Participate Form

Abuse Reporting Agreement (suspected abuse will be reported by volunteers)

Emergency Contact Form

Authorization for Release of Information (Department of Human Services performs a check on prospective volunteers for any reports of abuse)

Project Documentation

Pretest/interview

Posttest/interview

Attendance Sheet for parenting group meetings

Parent Partner Contact Sheet (records numbers and kinds of contacts between volunteer and participant: phone, face-to-face)

## Project Budget

Proper management of the budget assists the project in meeting its goals and objectives, just as a lack of attention to budget allocations jeopardizes its success. The budget is the means of accounting for all project expenditures. An effective budgeting system incorporates several key elements:

★ All program staff must understand the accounting system and the importance of remaining within the budget to reach overall program goals.

★ All budget-related activities should be controlled by clear policies and procedures.

★ Assign budget responsibilities to more than one person, with one person coordinating them to avoid error and to provide cross-check protection.

★ Timely, accurate, and understandable record keeping is essential.

★ Periodic review of the budget increases effective use of funds.

Accurate budgeting allows the project to avoid overspending and underspending. It is extremely difficult to satisfactorily achieve project goals and objectives if funds run short during the final stages of implementation. On the other hand, unused funds must be returned to the funder.

In the previous chapter, the project proposal outlined several budget categories. A general explanation of these categories, which can be used by most projects, is shown in Table 7.

Obvious miscalculations in the budget are looked upon unfavorably by the funder; therefore, carefully calculate the project's monetary expenditures without overeconomizing to the point of jeopardizing project operation and ending up with an embarrassing surplus.

# Staff Development and Training

## *Orientation*

Orientation is a familiarization process for staff, participants, and volunteers. Everyone benefits from gaining an understanding of their relationship to the program goals and objectives and the importance of their role in achieving them. Orientation for staff/volunteers may include the following:

★ An overview of the agency and the origin of the project

★ Roles of different staff persons

★ Rights/responsibilities of staff, volunteers, and participants

★ Project facilities, equipment, and use

## Table 7. The Project Budget

Every project budget should accurately enter any expenditures using categories similar to the ones that follow. Many funders have a specific list of budget categories and these should become the model for the project budget. Most budgets cover the following categories:

**Personnel**

| | |
|---|---|
| Administrative | Those who oversee the project operation or budget (e.g., project director, coordinator, or others). |
| Program staff | Those who participate in the operation of the project (e.g., curriculum specialist, parenting skills trainer, community liaison, volunteer coordinator, etc.). |
| Benefits | Generally, full-time personnel qualify for benefits such as social security, medical insurance, life insurance, etc., whereas part-time personnel benefit policies vary. |
| Consultants | Contracted persons or services to provide expertise in addition to staff expertise (e.g., contracts vary). |

**Nonpersonnel**

| | |
|---|---|
| Travel | Local travel rates follow the government or agency rate and include parking and tolls. Make separate categories for per diem, air fare (coach rate), or use of rental car or taxi. Associated costs such as gas, parking fees, etc., are also noted. Remember to ask for and keep receipts for all such expenditures. |
| Office supplies | Materials that are used for the project (e.g., paper, pens, etc.). |
| Phone/copying/ utilities/postage | Separate expenditures for long distance, installation, postage, or utilities that do not fall under indirect costs (e.g., office not at an agency). |
| Equipment | Purchase of items (e.g., cameras, computers, printers, tape recorders, etc.). Some funders either disallow or limit purchase of equipment. |
| Rental | Equipment is frequently leased or rented rather than purchased. Follow funder guidelines for this. |
| Office space | Separate office space, used by the project (that is not part of an agency), and is either rented or leased. |
| Copies/printing | Keep track of copies and charges, especially if this is not part of indirect costs. |
| Project materials | Educational, audiovisual, pamphlets, or other materials used as part of the program. |
| Miscellaneous | Any other items that do not fit the other categories (e.g., incentives for participant attendance). |
| Indirect costs | The host agency is reimbursed to provide services such as bookkeeping and payroll, space, and utilities. |
| In-kind | Services or materials provided by the project or agency as their contribution to operating costs. |

Orientation for participants may include the following:

★ Some information about the origin of the project

★ A description of the goals of the program (the goals should be worded positively and focus on benefits, such as strengthening the family or improving life skills, etc.)

★ Information about the content of the program

★ A review of the time frame for the program

★ Participant expectations of the program and participant responsibilities as part of the program

★ Information about incentives to participate or reimbursement for travel cost, etc.

## Training

To effectively deliver services to children and families at risk of maltreatment, it is beneficial for staff to receive training on a number of project-related topics. Training enables the staff to act in a legally and professionally responsible manner. Trained staff are also better able to provide the highest quality service, and as a result have a greater effect on reducing child maltreatment and helping families develop positive child-rearing practices.

Building in training experiences for project staff has the additional benefit of revealing worker strengths and weaknesses. Group training also provides an opportunity to use fellow workers as a support system in dealing with stress or as a resource for expertise. Furthermore, it is an aid in maintaining morale when staff are faced with different problems.

### Types of Training

**Preservice training:** Preservice training is provided before staff begin project work. All project staff without prior training should attend a training that covers the signs and symptoms of child maltreatment, reporting issues, and project procedures. Those staff or volunteers working directly with participants must have this training as a prerequisite to beginning work with participants.

**In-service training:** In-service training is provided at appropriate times during the course of the project. In-service training, scheduled as part of the regular work day or at other convenient times, may be the best way to reach the greatest number of staff. Training sessions can upgrade skills or introduce new procedures. It also is an opportunity for staff to exchange ideas and to get feedback. Schedule in-service training just prior to project activities that will benefit from staff having new or reviewed skills or updates in information.

**Continuing education:** Usually continuing education courses are offered by a local college or university or in conjunction with a local agency or state department. Attendance at these is an excellent way for project staff to fulfill licensing or certification requirements while increasing skills or receiving instruction about maltreatment-related topics.

**Staff meetings:** Although not a formal type of training, weekly staff meetings are an excellent means for project staff to inform each other of current developments, planned events, clerical priorities, etc. Minutes taken at meetings should be circulated so staff can review the information so as not to overlook important dates, times, events, etc.

More information about training is found in **Tool #7, Training**.

### How and When Should Staff Training Be Provided?
Depending on the number of staff, the scope of the project, the level of experience, and the different learning styles and educational background of the staff, a training agenda should select the topics that best add to the staff's ability to work with the target population. If the backgrounds of the staff are greatly different, training may have to be provided at different "levels" of content to be effective.

Providing training does not have to be expensive or involved. Use contacts at major agencies and health care and educational institutions to find out about trainings that are being offered locally. Identify those trainings that would best serve the project's training needs and schedule staff to attend.

A project can set up a "reciprocal program," calling upon a number of professionals in several agencies to present trainings within their area of expertise. This sharing of talent is a most effective arrangement, because it allows exposure to many perspectives and areas of expertise.

Trainings should be scheduled to predate the particular project activities that require the skills provided by the training. For instance, if a project is using an interviewing technique as part of its program, then staff or volunteers should receive interviewing training just prior to that phase of the project. Information that is critical to the work of the project should also be provided early on.

Some trainings are designed to enhance staff qualifications and expertise by presenting new research findings, adding to a knowledge base about a target population, or covering related topics such as current legislation. Schedule these trainings to fit into the project timeline at convenient times.

### Training Topics

The ability to recognize abuse and neglect is a critical part of the reporting process. The best ways of working with target populations who may have culturally different perceptions of abuse are also important issues. These and other issues and areas of information related to effective service delivery and achievement of project goals are the topics that project training should cover.

Each project will determine its training needs based on the level of experience and expertise of its staff. Some suggested topics follow. The topics with an asterisk are necessary for all projects.

★ *Project policies and procedures:

- Explain and review all project policies and procedures. Answer questions and provide reasons for the policies and procedures.

### *Legal Responsibility*

Mandatory reporting laws and regulations defining the process of reporting are in effect in every state. The reporting laws and procedures vary from state to state; therefore, it is essential that professionals and all prevention staff should be familiar with local, current reporting requirements. Contact the local Child Protection Service to obtain a copy of the state maltreatment law and to obtain information on reporting procedures. Inquire whether free training is available through Child Protection Services, as often there is a mandate to provide such training. See Table 8 for advice on how to develop and implement a policy.

★ *Reporting maltreatment (see Table 8 on page 116 for recommendations for projects on reporting maltreatment):

- Local laws and national guidelines and requirements (see box on next page)

- What response to expect from the local child protection service

- Reporting responsibilities, procedures, and project policy

★ *An overview of child abuse and neglect:

- Definitions

- Family dynamics, particularly of families in stress

- Indicators of maltreatment

- Child development

- Prevention strategies, with particular emphasis on the project methods

★ Skills (vary according to project):

- Interviewing parent/child

- Test administration

### Table 8. Developing a Reporting Policy

Clear procedures for reporting abuse are strongly recommended for every prevention project. (See Appendix F for a sample policy.) Recommendations for reporting maltreatment:

★ Procedures for how and when to make the report include the hotline number and notification of the administrator of the project when a report is made. The report should be specific and detailed, stated in simple terms. Program participants should be informed about the policy and sign an agreement of understanding.

★ Staff/volunteers should understand the social service process that follows maltreatment reports, as well as how to bypass "dead-ends" in the process if the results are unsatisfactory.

★ Staff should be familiar with referral possibilities for families.

★ Advocate for the child: the first responsibility is to report.

★ Before making a report, prepare a list of details (e.g., names, addresses, phone numbers, dates, places, descriptions) for the report.

★ Explain to participants up front that there is a reporting policy and that staff are legally responsible to make reports.

★ Always tell a participant when something is being reported, unless this is contraindicated by circumstances (e.g., additional harm to child, family will leave town, etc.). Tell them how and why it will be reported and then offer support.

★ If the Child Protective Services worker closes a case without adequate intervention, bring it to the attention of his/her supervisor. A letter detailing your concerns about the family may be more effective than a phone call.

Design an abuse report record form that contains spaces for the following elements or use the form as required by Child Protective Services (see Appendix F for a sample form):

★ The name of the person who takes the report at Child Protection Services, the name of the agency/department, and when the report was made

★ The name and address of the child

★ Age, birth date, and present whereabouts of the child

★ The name, phone number, and address of parent or adult responsible for the child, as well as his/her relationship to the child

★ The nature and description of the injury/incident. Include description of circumstances, evidence of previous injuries, or complaints that substantiate the current report or establish a cause

★ The signature of the person making the report, the date, and the name of any other persons notified, and the date of notification

- Accurate reporting and description/observation of data for records or program evaluation

★ Intercultural interaction:

- General communication skills

- Cultural awareness

- Specific information about working with the project's target population

- Practice in intercultural interaction

★ Stress management/time management:

- Alternative techniques or plans

- Practice or demonstration

★ Life style of low-income families:

- Attitude towards the service system

- Barriers to receiving service (e.g., lack of transportation, phone, child care, and/or literacy or other issues)

# Implementing the Program

## *Preparation of Project Materials*

Many projects will use, adapt, or develop project materials or curricula (e.g., educational pamphlets, posters, handouts, etc.) as part of their prevention program. All materials developed with public funds are considered "public domain" and may be freely reproduced. Copyrighted materials must be purchased or permission obtained for reproduction and distribution.

New or innovative materials developed by the project staff should be pilot tested before being applied under the actual project conditions. Pilot testing allows staff to check for appropriate reading level, language barriers, etc.

Many standardized evaluation materials (e.g., questionnaires, interview formats, psychological tests, etc.) can be confidently used without much preparation other than training in their proper use. (More information on measurement materials is found in Chapter 7, "Project Evaluation.") If the project situation varies substantially from the original application of these evaluation materials, however, then some adaptation may be necessary.

## The Program in Operation

Once the project framework is established, the materials are prepared and the staff (and volunteers) are oriented and trained, it is time to begin the actual prevention program. A responsive project continues to adapt and refine the program as needed. The following is an operational checklist:

★ Begin recruitment of program participants:

- Initiate referral agreements/arrangements with other agencies or organizations

- Initiate an advertising or media campaign

★ Organize/prepare support services if the project needs them:

- Coordinate transportation arrangements for participants to come to sessions, workshops, classes, etc.

- Arrange child care for participants

- Arrange for meals or other incentives

★ Complete intake or pretesting procedures:

- Administer pretests and/or collect completed permission or release forms

- Use feedback or information from intake or pretesting to make adaptations

★ Monitor the program through accurate and timely data collection and recording of information.

★ Analyze program data. (See Chapter 7, "Project Evaluation.")

★ Prepare a final report.

## Recruiting Participants

Recruitment of participants is frequently a critical factor in implementation unless a prevention project is school based, has prearranged referrals, or is otherwise incorporated into an existing program. Recruiting and retaining participants is particularly challenging for projects that are working with a difficult-to-access target population.

In general, prevention programs perceived as positive in their approach and that address barriers to attendance will be successful in recruiting participants and maintaining attendance.

### *Motivate*

The key to recruitment is motivation. It is essential to find out what motivates potential participants. Sometimes the best way to determine what it will take to get people to attend the program is to ask them. Successful programs discover what is needed to get people to participate and then design the program accordingly. For instance, adolescent parents who are out of school, live with parents, and have few socializing opportunities may be eager to socialize with other adolescents as part of a prevention program, especially if their own parents will watch the children.

### *Reduce Barriers*

Some individuals have more than one barrier to overcome and need multiple motivators. Sometimes hidden pressures from peers or family members are the barriers to participation. Adolescent parents who are still in school may be reluctant to be identified as "parents" by their school peers and therefore may not want to become part of a parenting program, especially a school-based program.

See Case #17 for an example of combining methods to recruit participants.

## Case #17: Combining Methods to Recruit Participants

The **Single Parent Project**, Cuyahoga County, Ohio, targeted minority single parent families.

The director of the project had previous experience in working with this population and knew that recruitment had to be done face-to-face. Direct, verbal contact with potential participants through a door-to-door campaign established initial interest in the program. Each person contacted was left a colorful flyer employing graphics to draw attention to the information. The highlights of the program were listed, as well as dates, times, locations, phone numbers, etc., for easy reference.

This method of recruitment proved to be more successful than either flyers sent alone to potential participants with no preliminary face-to-face contact or flyers sent to other community agencies and directors seeking referrals.

### Incentives

Some projects have successfully used incentives in attracting participants and for maintaining attendance. Items such as a notepad or key chain with positive messages or providing a meal for parents who attend a session at a time when a meal would be missed can be surprisingly helpful. Incentives, however, should be used with caution. First of all, incentives may be expensive, and the program may actually suffer if at some point incentives are no longer able to be provided. Secondly, incentives should be used with restraint to prevent any possible clouding of program effects due to the use of incentives (e.g., participants' responses to questionnaires, interviews, or evaluation questions are not candid or are deliberately positive because the incentives influence the response).

### Recruitment Issues

Is it ethical to disguise the real goal of the project, the prevention of child maltreatment, when presenting the program to a target population that was selected precisely because it is at risk of maltreatment? Being candid about the purpose of the program with participants may mean that they will not return. These are serious issues and cannot be minimized. It is fair, however, to present the benefits of a positive "parenting" or "life skills" program or any other program to participants without emphasizing that is also an abuse prevention program. Avoid attaching the stigma of "high risk" to participants. It is important to remember that being "at risk" is not a predetermination of maltreatment. Many participants choose to learn positive skills because they are already aware of the risks for maltreatment in their daily circumstances. It is best to stress the positive aspects of the program but also to answer participant questions honestly. (See Table 9 on page 122.)

# Public Relations and Community Support

Any prevention project benefits from promoting a positive image. Investing some work and energy into developing a good public relations program brings rewards in several ways.

## *Benefits of Promoting the Project*

★ Increased public awareness about maltreatment issues encourages support for prevention programs.

★ It is easier to recruit participants and volunteers with a known and positive image.

★ It is easier to generate donations of goods or services to use as incentives or supports for the project.

★ Good publicity about a project's work helps in obtaining continued funding.

Actively soliciting community collaboration in the initiation and implementation of prevention programs both empowers and delegates responsibility for preventing child maltreatment. As a result, prevention becomes an individual and community objective and contributors gain a sense of accomplishment and belief in their ability to effect change.

### Table 9. What Works in Recruiting and Retaining Participants

★ Publicize using local newspapers, church bulletin boards, or short presentations before a variety of audiences. Customize the approach or message to fit the audience.

**Note:** Place advertisements near other positive advertisements in adult/community education mail-outs or publications.

★ Use a poster and/or brochure or handouts and greet people going to classes, meetings, or other places where likely participants go. Use short, catchy messages that the target population can relate to.

★ Develop contacts with cooperating community service providers and ask for referrals.

★ Emphasize culturally specific aspects of the program. Show how the program is different.

★ Make use of available media community service time.

★ Offer to give parenting tips or answer questions on a talk show and tell about the project and how to participate as well.

★ Emphasize the positive benefits of the program.

★ Choose a project name and meeting place that is positive, nonoffensive, and does not carry any identification with agencies or groups that would make participants feel stigmatized (e.g., holding a program called M.O.M.S. in school for adolescent mothers clearly identifies them as mothers when they may not want to be so identified).

★ Plan program sessions to be part of another activity (e.g., an outing, a speaker, a movie, etc.).

★ Program recognition is important in drawing and retaining participants. When several sources (e.g., doctor, social worker, other participant, etc.) mention a program, it becomes known.

★ Provide transportation, food, child care, or supervised play group for children, bilingual staff, or volunteers to help overcome barriers.

★ Combining a parent program with a children's program encourages parents to attend to keep the child in the children's program.

★ Use incentives such as meals, gift certificates, outings, etc.

★ Don't schedule sessions in conflict with other events (e.g., first of the month/public assistance checks are distributed, free clinic hours, local church or other organization events, etc.).

In particular, a program initiated from within the community has a distinct advantage in using the expertise of the community leaders in implementing the project. Fostering communication with key persons from the target population improves the likelihood of getting their cooperation in meeting the population's need. See Case #18 for an example of how good promotion pays off in benefits for a project.

Projects that establish community advisory groups enjoy a triple benefit by formalizing public support and visibility for the project, using the group for valuable feedback and employing the vitality, experience, and expertise of members as bonus resources.

### Case #18: Seeking Community Support

The **Child Assault Prevention Project** (CAP), Summit County, Ohio, a primary prevention project providing workshops and training for children, parents, and professionals, was unknown in its new target area. As a means of getting exposure, the project formed an advisory council for support. The advisory council was made up of professional people with community contacts and parents representing various child-focused programs (e.g., scouts, church groups, etc.). The council primarily functioned as 1) an advocacy group, 2) a source of ideas and implementation of fundraising events (i.e., auction and dinner), and 3) a planning and evaluation group.

The members of the council were able to communicate to the community the need for the project and verified the project staff's credentials, thus laying the positive groundwork for implementing the project.

## Planning and Budgeting for Good Public Relations

The well-designed project has planned ahead to build community appreciation for the project's prevention work by including public relations activities into the project's management and operational plan. Each project, however, should plan its public contact in relation to its scope and budget and the benefits of the publicity for the project:

★ Make a checklist of audiences that are important to the project.

★ Prepare a calendar for public relations activities and updates.

★ Plan the public relations activities to coincide with other community events (e.g., health fairs, elections, school events, etc.).

★ List key contacts who should be periodically informed of the project's progress and select a method of informing them (e.g., newsletter, phone call, meeting).

### Set Public Relations Objectives

★ To raise awareness among the target population about the project's service(s) (e.g., short promotional presentations at local churches, civic groups, school functions, or wherever the target population congregates). Use key contacts to gain entrance.

★ To increase general public awareness of maltreatment issues (e.g., offer to answer questions or give advice on local media talk shows in exchange for a chance to promote the project or prevention messages; capitalize on an incident or news event related to child abuse and offer comments or interviews).

★ To reach a larger audience with short impact messages (e.g., posters, flyers, displays, photos, newsletter, etc.).

★ To advocate by providing legislators in local, state, and federal positions with information (e.g., letters, petitions, etc.).

★ To educate the public about the difference between discipline and maltreatment or about the long-term effects of maltreatment (e.g., use pamphlets, talks, flyers, displays, tapes/videos, photos, etc.).

### Budgeting for Public Relations

Time and expense invested in public relations can be minimized if priorities are set to fit a fixed budget. Project planners or staff can brainstorm a list of possible public relations activities or methods along with the cost in time and expense of materials for each. They can list the expected benefits for the suggestions and make selections that show the most public relations value for the particular project.

Use donated time and services to fuel the public relations program. It may be possible to find a volunteer to coordinate the public relations program as well as find sponsors to finance it. This is a fun and rewarding job for the right volunteer. Printing costs or use of equipment can often be obtained through donations in return for mentioning the donor. Special events are good opportunities to enlist the sponsorship of local businesses in return for high visibility on all printed materials or broadcast announcements.

### Evaluate the Public Relations Program

Build in the means of obtaining feedback from the public by including contact names and phone numbers on all printed materials or media announcements. Ask callers where they heard about the project. Record comments to use as evaluation data.

### Which Public Relations Methods Should a Project Use?

Select and use public relations tools that best serve the needs of the program. Every project should have a fact sheet, presenting an overview of the project so that the general public can quickly grasp the importance or the project's goals. There are many media available to promote the project. See **Tool #8, Public Relations Tools for Prevention Projects**, for more information on the types and uses of different media.

## Completing the Implementation Process

The project affects many people beyond the target group. Staff, volunteers, and the community are all enriched by the hope-filled messages of caring and empathy that inspire the daily functions of the project.

Working with prevention issues and with populations experiencing multiple disadvantages can be difficult and frustrating. It is important to take the time to highlight the victories and consciously identify the successes of the project. At regular intervals, ask participants, staff, volunteers, advisory group members, and others who are in contact with the program to note positive observations or experiences. Provide a variety of means for everyone connected with the project to express themselves (e.g., informal discussions, anonymously written comments, etc.). This puts the emphasis on the good changes that are occurring and reduces the negative influences.

The different elements of the implementation process are now synchronized to meet the needs the project has targeted. Due to the conscientious investment of time and effort in assessment and design stages, the project is now able to deliver a healthy, functioning prevention program.

A significant component of an effective prevention project is evaluation. A successful project requires the inclusion of sound evaluation methods to demonstrate its impact on reducing maltreatment and to contribute to the efficacy of future prevention projects. The next chapter covers evaluation topics and issues and describes how to incorporate this essential component into the project.

## References

Ash, G. (1986). *Resources for staff development & training*. Cleveland, OH: Child Day Care Planning Project.

Broadhurst, D. D., & MacDicken, R. A. (1979). *Training in the prevention and treatment of child abuse and neglect*. [DHEW Publication No. (OHDS) 79-30201]. Available from the National Center on Child Abuse and Neglect, P.O. Box 1182, Washington, D.C. 20013.

The Community Training Unit of the New Jersey Division of Youth and Family Services. (1984). *A curriculum on child abuse and neglect for New Jersey school personnel*. Trenton, NJ: Family Life Development Center, Child Protective Services Training Institute, Cornell University.

Conners, T. D. (Ed.). (1980). *The nonprofit organization handbook*. New York: McGraw-Hill.

Dorman, R., & Rollo, K. (Eds.). (1985). *Preventing child abuse in the harvest: A handbook for migrant educators*. Available from Migrant Education Unit, Office of General Education, New York State Education Department, Albany, NY 12234.

Drucker, P. F. (1990). *Managing the non-profit organization: Practices and principles.* New York: Harper Collins Publishers.

Larkin, R. F. (1984, June). Financial care and feeding of the non-profit organization. *The Virginia Accountant Quarterly.* Reprint.

Minnesota Office on Volunteer Services. (1984). *Volunteer for Minnesota: Community handbook, part 2.* Available from Minnesota Office on Volunteer Services, Department of Administration, 500 Rice Street, St. Paul, MN 55155.

National Information Center on Volunteerism. (1985). *Partnership and volunteerism: Effective utilization of community involvement.* Presented at 19th National Migrant Education Conference in Atlanta, Georgia. Available from National Information Center on Volunteerism, P.O. Box 4179, Boulder, CO 80306.

Sneed, R. H. Providing child protective services to culturally diverse families. In U.S. Department of Health and Human Services, *Perspectives on child maltreatment in the mid '80s* (pp. 31-32). [DHHS Publication No. (OHDS) 84-30338]. Washington, DC: U.S. Government Printing Office.

U.S. Department of Health, Education, and Welfare. (1980, June). *How to plan and carry out a successful public awareness program on child abuse and neglect.* [DHHS Publication No. (OHDS) 80-30089]. Washington, DC: U.S. Government Printing Office.

Weiss, W. H. (1980). *Supervisor's standard reference handbook.* Englewood Cliffs, NJ: Prentice-Hall.

# Project Evaluation

There are service providers who work fearlessly in high crime areas, delve into the most personal issues with uncooperative families, and do battle with the frustrating bureaucracies of public agencies—but who quiver at the mention of the word "evaluation." Why should evaluation evoke feelings of fear, incompetence, or even anger in service providers?

There are probably several reasons. Some may perceive it as a burden that saps resources from services but produces no real benefits. Others may be intimidated by the terminology or the statistics. Still others may wonder whether their job may be on the line if the results are not positive. Sadly, these attitudes often prevent service providers from including a sound evaluation in their program design.

While it's true that a poorly executed evaluation will produce no real benefits to anyone, a well-done evaluation is an integral aspect of any successful prevention program and can inform every aspect of the program, from improving referral sources to maintaining program participation. It is unfortunate that service providers often view evaluation as a "necessary evil," rather than as the avenue to improving services and demonstrating their success to a wide audience.

In addition to the programmatic reasons for evaluation, there are increasing pressures from funders and policymakers who are calling for more accountability in the human services and who are unwilling to support programs lacking a strong evaluation component. At the same time, experts in the field express concern that we do not have "tried and true" prevention models with demonstrable outcomes, because rigorous evaluation designs have not been a component of most programs. Fink and McCloskey [1990] reviewed a number of high profile prevention programs and found their evaluations lacking on four key points: inadequate definition of child abuse and neglect, lack of valid instruments, no conclusions regarding which type of families benefited most from the programs, and omission of cost-benefit analysis.

Even federally funded demonstration programs intended to develop child abuse prevention models for dissemination have encountered difficulties in implementing successful evaluation plans. As a result, federal demonstration grants are now required to have an outside evaluator and spend at least 15% of their budget on evaluation [CSR, Inc. 1997].

It's not surprising then that grassroots efforts, which comprise the majority of prevention programs, have likewise had weak evaluation components. Working with a limited staff and budget, resources are usually focused upon service delivery rather than evaluation. Yet, without a sound evaluation, service providers cannot tell whether the program made a positive difference for the participants or even identify whether the program delivered the amount, type, or quality of services specified in the program objectives.

Service providers may believe that, because child abuse prevention programs are *intended* to help people, that they do. But without evaluation, that belief rests upon the personal opinions of participants and providers. Anecdotal evidence provides a human face to statistical results but cannot stand alone as proof of program impact.

In sum, an evaluation can demonstrate program effectiveness, show results for dollars spent, allow you to compare the effectiveness of an intervention with different populations, and identify unforeseen barriers to service delivery.

This chapter provides an overview of the evaluation process specifically as it relates to child maltreatment prevention with a focus on describing common difficulties encountered in conducting an evaluation of a community-based project.

CONTACT INFORMATION: Bill Trochim's Center for Social Research Methods is a great on-line resource for information on applied social research methods. Go to *http://trochim.human.cornell.edu/*.

## Hiring a Consultant

The first step for a prevention project that does not have in-house expertise in evaluation is to hire a consultant. When doing so, you must be careful to find someone who understands how to conduct evaluation within the real-life community context and who respects the ideas and opinions of program staff. A collaborative and positive working relationship between the evaluator and the staff is key to designing an evaluation that will be able to produce results and answer questions that will assist staff in improving the program. Perhaps the only thing sadder than a program without an effective evaluation is an evaluation report that is not used to improve a program because it is not relevant [Patton 1978].

The local university is probably a good place to start in your quest for this practical evaluator, but there may be private consultants, consulting firms, or a nonprofit agency with considerable evaluation expertise. The credential most important to consider in making your selection is not the evaluator's affiliation, but his or her track record of successful evaluations and satisfied customers. After a preliminary meeting, a potential consultant should be able to provide you with a general idea of the type of evaluation that would be conducted and a price estimate. It may be a good idea to request that the consultant provide a "menu of options" and prices for different types of evaluation activities that could be conducted. The client agency decides what best meets their needs and budget.

Whether or not an outside evaluator or a staff person takes charge of the evaluation, the steps are essentially the same. Make sure to hold regular staff meetings to discuss the progress of the evaluation and any problems that may have arisen, particularly with regards to data collection. If problems are not addressed in a timely fashion, then the entire evaluation can go off course.

## Step 1: Determine the Goals of the Evaluation

Evaluation goals should correspond to program goals and should be developed as part of the overall program planning process. It is important to consider who wants the evaluation results and how they will use them. Funders, public officials, agency directors, project directors, and line workers may all have somewhat different agendas. The funder may want to ensure that the services have reached the targeted population; public officials may want to determine if the program has saved money by eliminating the need for other services; agency directors may want to know whether the project is cost effective to run; the project director may want to know if the program made a positive impact on participants; and line workers may want to know whether the services they provided were well received by clients.

All of these can be answered by a comprehensive evaluation. You must look at the project resources, however, and determine what is feasible to accomplish given time, staff, expertise, equipment, barriers to data collection, and budget. Set realistic goals that can be accomplished well. It is wise to include components that evaluate the impact of the project (i.e., outcome evaluation) and describe how the project was implemented (i.e., process evaluation). If resources are tight, it is best to streamline both of these components, rather than omit one.

PROJECT EVALUATION ★ **133**

If the program is in its pilot phase, then the process evaluation is extremely important, so that the program content and implementation can be adjusted if outcomes are not positive. The pilot phase should allow for some "midcourse corrections" to improve the program model, as illustrated in Case #19.

### Case #19: Adjusting During the Pilot Phase

The original design of **Parenting Plus** in Cleveland, Ohio, was to match high-risk mothers with senior volunteers from within the mothers' own neighborhoods to offer information and support. During the first year of the pilot, however, it was determined that finding large numbers of appropriate volunteers to meet the needs of the target population was not feasible. In addition, finding appropriate "matches" between mother and senior also proved quite difficult. Process evaluation revealed that many of the seniors wanted to "tell the mothers what to do," rather then empower them, which was the project goal. Data from the mothers indicated that they were sometimes antagonistic toward the seniors because of this attitude.

In Year II, parents were matched with other parents from within their parenting skills groups. These parent/partner dyads were quite successful and reinforced the empowerment philosophy of the program while eliminating the need for recruiting volunteers, which had been a huge drain on project resources.

## The Evaluation "Mystique"

Program staff often have some fears or concerns about the evaluation. Attitudes span the gamut from those who feel threatened to those that feel it is simply extra paperwork and perceive no benefit to the program. These attitudes can undermine the evaluation either directly, because records are not kept or data not collected, or indirectly, because forms are not filled out seriously. Without staff buy-in at every level, the evaluation can easily be compromised.

Evaluation has a certain mystique for people who have no training in research methodology. Demystify the evaluation by bringing everyone into the process. Ask for opinions and consider them in making up the evaluation plan. At times even the project director may feel intimidated by the process, especially if an outside consultant is hired to conduct the evaluation. The outside evaluator should rely upon project staff and other stakeholders to set the agenda for the evaluation. Otherwise, the evaluation may not address the issues considered significant by the individuals who would most benefit from the information.

Stress how evaluation will help the project staff do their jobs better. Explain how the process evaluation will provide staff with valuable information to improve the project, document how they work with families, identify obstacles they face in delivering services, and provide a way for them to make changes in the project. Have all staff involved in generating questions for the evaluation to address. Make sure that each person perceives the benefit of the evaluation.

## Step 2: Design the Evaluation Plan

The evaluation design specifies the manner in which the evaluation will be conducted. It identifies the subjects of the evaluation, data to be collected, and specifies the circumstances and controls necessary for a sound evaluation to be conducted.

The scope of the evaluation, the timeline, and the budget must be outlined. Determining the number of participants to be served is obviously dependent upon resources such as staff, timeline, and budget. Serving a small number of clients will make it more difficult to demonstrate statistically significant effects, however. There are statistical calculations to guide you in determining the needed sample size to obtain a certain desired effect size. If you do have some flexibility in determining sample size, it may be a good idea to check with a statistician who can do a power calculation and give you some guidance on this matter.

The final choice of a design balances the goals of the project, the needs of those who want evaluation results, and the resources of the project. Make sure that you allot enough funds to conduct the evaluation you've planned. Remember that it could be the deciding factor in whether your project maintains continued funding. A sound evaluation will both describe how the program operated, as well judge the impact it made. The "how" is tapped by a process evaluation, while impact is measured through an outcome evaluation.

## Process Evaluation

Conducting a process evaluation is a systematic way to collect data that describe how the project was implemented. It addresses such questions as the following:

★ Who gave referrals?

★ Who participated, who refused services, and who dropped out of services?

★ Who was present at the home visit? Were they disruptive?

★ Did the participants fit the description of the target population?

★ How did staff implement the curriculum?

★ How much did they deviate from planned content?

★ What did families think about the services? Were they accessible?

★ Are some staff more effective than others? Why?

Surprisingly, many programs do not collect basic information about how services were utilized, and many others collect some data but not in a systematic fashion [Jacobs 1988]. Although these data cannot tell us the effect of the services on clients, they still serve an important function. First, they demonstrate accountability to the funder. As Jacobs states, "A program, however small, should be able to report that, in a particular time period, X number of families were provided Y amount of service at a cost of Z" [Jacobs 1988, p. 56].

Generally, projects design their own process evaluation forms, since they are project specific. Listed below are some "generic" process forms and the types of information they typically contain.

★ **Intake form:** Includes referral source, referral date, demographic and background information, identified risk factors present, specific needs of the client, client expectations about the program, and perceived barriers to participating (e.g. transportation).

★ **Service plan:** Includes goals for the family, services the family currently receives, and plan to reach those goals. It is updated at set intervals regarding progress made toward goals.

★ **Contact form:** Each phone or in-person contact with the client or on behalf of the client is recorded. Notes of what transpired, date, length of time, and other people present can be included.

★ **Attendance form:** Includes participant attendance or absence at group meetings or home visits.

★ **Staff assessment form:** Staff rate the effectiveness of the group meeting or home visit. Scales could include amount of client participation, client reaction to material discussed, etc.

## Fine-Tuning the Program

It may take some time for new programs to adjust services before a positive impact can be demonstrated in an outcome evaluation. During this start-up period, the process data can demonstrate that the program is able to reach and enroll families and deliver services, providing some credibility to the program. A funder is likely to allow some time to make programmatic changes.

It is crucial to document exactly how line workers are implementing the program. Even when there is a detailed curriculum, each person will put his or her individual stamp on it. It is important for the project director to keep lines of communication open so that staff feel comfortable sharing their own style of implementation and to develop ways to document them. A form could be developed on which the group leader notes how each session went and documents specific deviations from the planned session.

For example, a parenting class may be focused on teaching *time-out* to parents at Session Three, but some parents challenge time-out as a viable technique. Most of the session is spent talking about physical punishment and why parents believe that it is better than *time-out*. The group leader decides that she needs to jump ahead in the curriculum to pull in material from the session on physical punishment and is able to address many of the concerns raised by participants. If she has a way to document this, then it will be possible to compare her experience with that of other group leaders and determine whether there is a pattern and the curriculum needs to be altered.

## Outcome Evaluation

An effective outcome evaluation measures the degree of change (if any) brought about by the project services. Therefore, a comparison must be made to some baseline condition, attitude, or behavior present at intake. Thus a pretest/posttest design is used with pretest data collected prior to providing services to the participant and posttest data collected after the final service contact. In addition, it is advisable to collect follow-up data at some point after the termination of services. For example, you may be concerned that, without the support of program staff, old attitudes and behaviors will re-emerge, especially if other people in the caregiver's environment do not endorse the "new" attitudes of the participant.

Follow-up data illustrate whether immediate postprogram gains are maintained, lost, or even magnified over a certain period of time after services have ceased. Six-month or one-year follow-ups are common intervals of time for data collection. The longer the time interval, the more impressive it is that results have been sustained, but the harder it may be to find the participants.

## Choosing Outcome Measures

It is crucial when deciding what to measure that you resist the temptation to measure everything upon which the project might have an effect. Always remember that the time, patience, and motivation of staff and participants must be considered when deciding on the number of forms, questionnaires, and surveys to include. It may seem a wonderful idea in the planning stage to measure self-esteem, knowledge of child development, social support, child-rearing attitudes, and stress level. But consider whether parents (especially highly stressed ones) would be willing to sit down and fill out forms for two hours. And even if they'll do it once, it will be even harder to get them to sit down and do it a second time after the program is over.

Choose outcome measures wisely. Focus on specific changes the program is supposed to make in participants, and ignore other things that you think may be affected. One significant result sounds better than a laundry list of mostly nonsignificant ones. When you "throw in the kitchen sink," you're likely to get nonsignificant results. It is much more impressive to say that the program significantly decreases parents' use of physical punishment, than to say that the program doesn't decrease stress, improve self-esteem, or increase social support, but does decrease parents use of physical punishment. And if that's really the one thing your program is attempting to do, then you undermine the program's success by measuring lots of possible peripheral effects. Demonstrating significant change in people is not easy, and "fishing expeditions" are usually not successful.

## Use Standardized Measures

It is not advisable for project staff to develop new outcome measures, since they will generally not have the resources to establish reliability and validity of the measures. Using standardized measures with proven reliability and validity is preferable from a methodological perspective and is actually less work for service providers. Sometimes instruments come in both a long and short version. Usually, the long version is developed first and then a shorter version is adapted from it to provide a briefer alternative. If the short version is valid and reliable and measures the key dimensions that you are seeking to change, then use it.

In some instances, standardized instruments come with normative data that provide reference points for scores on the instrument with percentile rankings for both the general and special populations. This is useful for establishing the baseline risk level of the target population. For example, using the Parental Stress Index, it possible to determine the percentile ranking of the stress score for each participant. It is powerful to be able to state that, at intake, "80% of participants had a stress level higher than 75% of the general population." This establishes the high-risk nature of the population quantitatively.

## Locating Outcomes Measures

It is extremely rare for child abuse prevention projects to use actual incidence rates of substantiated cases of maltreatment as the outcome measure. Although this is the most powerful evidence of impact, it is fraught with difficulties. Instead most projects turn to "paper and pencil" assessment measures. Since there is no single reason why maltreatment occurs and projects may attempt to influence any one of a number of risk factors, there are a number of ways in which projects attempt to assess effectiveness. Child-rearing attitudes, self-esteem, parent's perception of the child, knowledge of child development, use of coping strategies, stress level, family interaction patterns, and conflict management skills are some of the areas that programs may try to assess.

There are numerous resources for locating assessment measures. Some measures are "public domain" and can be reproduced freely without cost. Many are copyrighted and must be obtained from the author or publisher at a fee. Some authors allow adaptation of their instrument by others, and some will not allow it—but it is always worth a phone call to find out. (See a listing of resources at the end of this chapter.)

Two measures bear mentioning specifically because they are directly relevant to populations at risk for abuse, have demonstrated validity and reliability, have scales to detect respondents who may be answering in a questionable fashion, and provide normative data that indicate percentile rankings for scores in well-defined populations.

The Child Abuse Potential Inventory [Milner 1986] is a measure that was developed to screen individuals for being physical abusers. It contains three validity scales (lie scale, random responding, inconsistency) that allow you to identify respondents with questionable scores and has a cutoff score above which the participant is highly likely to be physically abusive. Validation studies indicate that it is quite accurate (though not infallible) in terms of correctly identifying parents who are abusive. Although not originally developed to be used as an outcome measure, it has been used as one successfully [Milner 1986].

The Parental Stress Index [Abidin 1995] was developed to identify parent-child systems under excessive stress and can be used with parents of children as young as 1 month. It also contains a defensive responding scale to identify those parents who may be responding defensively so that their scores can be interpreted with caution.

## Using Child Protective Services Data

The most direct outcome measure is derived by searching the local or state child protective services (CPS) database to determine whether the parent has been the perpetrator of a substantiated case of abuse or neglect. This can be done by a search of CPS records, but requires consent from the participants if you are to receive case-specific information. Another approach is for the child protection agency to give you back only the number and type of cases within the program and control groups without any identifying information. In this way confidentiality is not breached, and you can determine whether the group effects were significant. However, you lose case-specific data.

The quality of the data in the child protection database is another issue. First, of course, is the fact that not all cases are reported. Ironically, your program staff may make a number of child abuse reports on families in the program and thereby increase the incidence of officially recognized maltreatment among program participants. Since families in a comparison group are not in close contact with program staff, they are not as likely to be reported even though the actual incidence of abuse may be the same or higher in that group [Olds & Kitzman 1993].

Before embarking on a plan to use CPS data, it is crucial to meet with staff that manage the official database to understand how records are kept, what type of identifying information is needed to search records, and what type of information they will be able to provide to you about a substantiated case. In some states records are kept locally, while in others there is a state registry.

Finally, be aware that even though child abuse is widespread, it still is a relatively rare occurrence. Unless you have a relatively large sample size, it will be nearly impossible to detect a statistically significant decrease in abuse after the program ends.

Having cited these difficulties, it is still important to note that using substantiated cases as an outcome measure is probably the most powerful evidence of success you can provide. A handful of programs have utilized CPS data and not found a reduction in incidence rate [Olds & Kitzman 1993]. The major exception is the Prenatal/Early Infancy Project, which is currently held as "the gold standard" in child abuse prevention evaluation methods and results. Using CPS data, they were able to demonstrate reduced incidence in the program group long after the program ended [Olds et al. 1997].

## Control/Comparison Groups

Control groups are an accepted and widely used feature of clinical research in medicine and psychology and allow the investigator to ascertain whether a certain "experimental" treatment is beneficial, detrimental, or has no impact on the patient. Likewise in prevention programming, randomly assigning families to the program or to a control group is the most rigorous manner of conducting an evaluation. Results achieved with this design provide the strongest evidence that the prevention program and not some other factor is responsible for the positive change observed.

The control group should resemble the program group both in terms of demographic characteristics (age, race, marital status, and sex) and key psychological characteristics (e.g., motivation to be in the program). Ideally, once you obtain the parents' consent to participate in the project, you then assign them to either the control or program group, having explained that the assignment to groups is totally by chance. It does not always follow, however, that you will be believed. In one project conducted by Applewood Centers, staff heard through the grapevine that some mothers believed that group assignment was based on how you performed on the pretest measure. If you "passed" you went into the control group since you "didn't need help," but if you flunked, you went into the program group to receive the help you needed.

Despite the methodological advantage of using a control or comparison group, it is the rare prevention program that has used such a group in its evaluation design. There are several difficulties that may account for this. First is the allocation of resources. Establishing a control group and collecting data from them takes considerable resources. Unless mandated by the funder, programs usually put their resources elsewhere. Program eligibility is another factor. You may simply not be able to deny services to certain families because of public policy or law. Finally, comes the issue of ethics and "withholding treatment" from high-risk families. There are several ways to address this issue without compromising the evaluation:

★ **Develop a waiting list for services**. Assess people upon entry to the waiting list, then again just prior to providing services to them, and, finally, at the program's end. (The time period between each data collection point should be fairly consistent across participants.) If data indicate no changes in the group after being on the waiting list, but a significant change after receiving the program, there is strong evidence that the program has been effective.

★ **Provide some extra service to families they would not otherwise receive, but that should not affect the ability to tease**

**out major program effects**. For example, the Prenatal Early Infancy Project [Olds et al. 1997] randomly assigned pregnant women to one of four groups with varying levels of services. Group 1 received developmental screening for their child; Group 2 received developmental screening plus transportation to medical appointments; Group 3 received all of the Group 2 services, plus a nurse who made home visits during pregnancy; and Group 4 received all of Group 3 services, and the nurse continued to visit until the child reached age 2.

★ **Compare families receiving your special program with families receiving "regular" services**. For example, the Parenting Plus project in Cleveland, Ohio [Dorman & Spottsville 1994] randomly assigned Head Start mothers to one of three groups: Group 1 received regular Head Start support services, Group 2 attended parenting groups, and Group 3 attended parenting groups and were assigned a parent partner for support.

(A note about terminology: the terms *control group* and *comparison group* are sometimes used interchangeably. The connotation of a control group, however, is that the members receive absolutely no services, while membership in a comparison group usually means that the individuals have received some type of service, but not the treatment under scrutiny.)

## Step 3: Data Collection

The best evaluation plan is worthless if data collection does not result in a complete, high-quality data set. Evaluators sometimes make the mistake of setting the data collection in motion and then sitting back and waiting for the word that it's complete. Too late they'll discover that forms have been filled out incorrectly or not at all, that some participants complete the "pretest" after they've been in the program for awhile, or that most participants can't be located to administer the posttest.

To avoid these pitfalls, a realistic data collection plan must be put into place and monitored regularly. Staff working with the families may be able to identify up front the barriers to data collection and which factors will cause participant attrition. The following issues should be considered, so that appropriate measures can be taken to deal with them.

★ What is the reading level of participants?

★ What is the illiteracy rate?

★ How many families have no phones?

★ How many have no reliable mailing address?

★ How often families do move?

★ How do families in the community view the program evaluation?

★ Where and when is it best to collect data?

★ Should incentives be used? What type?

★ How should the evaluation be explained to participants?

## Training Data Collectors

Here are some suggestions for gathering accurate and complete data.

★ Whoever is given the responsibility of collecting data from participants—be they students, volunteers, or staff—must be thoroughly trained in how to correctly administer the instruments.

★ Whenever feasible, it is optimal for those collecting data to be "blind" with respect to group assignment. If not, the possibility of bias is introduced, but will be less of a factor if instruments are in a self-report format and require no ratings by the data collector.

★ Provide instruction about general data collection procedures (how to explain the purpose of the evaluation, how to establish rapport, what to do in cases of resistance or refusal, how to handle a literacy problem).

★ Provide specific instructions about the administration of each instrument. Include practice in administering the measure and recording data in a role-playing format.

★ Encourage the immediate reporting of any irregularities in the data collection, such as spouses conferring with each other as they complete the forms, children distracting the parent, etc.

★ Stress the need for confidentiality in all aspects of data collection.

★ Provide evaluation folders holding all the forms for each participant and a checklist on the front to ensure that all data is collected.

Program staff may have a hard time with the concept of a control group that receives less in the way of services. It might be especially difficult for them to be placed in the position of explaining to the staff of other community agencies why a control group is necessary. It may be wise to identify a specially trained staff person with evaluation expertise to be the project representative to the community.

## Concerns of Participants Regarding Data Collection

Program participants have no personal investment in filling out evaluation forms. They are looking for help, not paperwork. Many are fed up with filling out government forms and some may be intimidated by forms that look like school tests. The evaluator is well-served by putting him- or herself into the shoes of the participant having to fill out forms. A *Consent to Participate Form* should be clear in describing both the services that the program will provide to the participant and the responsibilities of the participant including program attendance, forms to be completed, and incentives to be provided (if any). Listed below are some of the ideas that you may encounter in participants and how your staff can handle those beliefs so that the evaluation is not undermined.

> *This information could be used against me. I could lose government benefits, agency services, or even my children.*

In the *Consent to Participate Form*, make clear to the participants that no data will be shared with other agencies and, whenever possible, place no names on any forms. Use ID numbers to preserve anonymity. Make sure parents understand the role of the project in the community and differentiate it from the role of official agencies. You will have to report parents if you suspect child abuse and neglect, but this information is likely to come from firsthand observation, rather than from anything written on a form.

*You'll think (find out) I'm a bad parent/bad person.*

Normalize the difficulties of being a parent and the need for all parents to have help available. Emphasize that the *program* is being evaluated, not the participants, and how the information is used to see if the program is helpful to parents.

*I don't understand what this says or how to fill this out, but I don't want to admit it.*

Pilot test questionnaires to make sure parents don't misinterpret certain questions. For example, one project asked parents' to name their children's strengths on a pretest and a number of parents responded regarding the child's physical strength instead of his talents and abilities. Thus, the agency reworded the question to explain what they meant by "strengths."

### Use of Incentives

It can be helpful to include some material incentives to participants and to comparison group members for completion of evaluation instruments. This can be presented as a gift of appreciation for the parent's time and effort. When working with low-income populations, giving cash is usually not advisable. The data collector does not want to be known as someone who is carrying around sums of cash in high crime rate neighborhoods. Checks may be difficult for people to cash. Gift certificates to local fast food restaurants or grocery stores, household items, infant supplies such as diapers, or toys and books for children are all possible options.

## Data from Staff

Staff are invested in providing services, not collecting data. Show staff that you are attempting to make the evaluation as easy for them as possible. Have staff involved in the design of forms they will complete. Make the paperwork user friendly. Give prompts such as checklists or reminders to help them collect data on time. Build data collection procedures into the operating procedures of the project whenever possible. For example, referral and/or intake forms can be designed to include demographic information, risk factors, and other information for the evaluation.

# Step 4: Data Analysis

Analyzing data requires some expertise. If you have hired a consultant to help design the evaluation, that person should also help with the analysis. Make sure that s/he is able to describe the meaning of the results in layperson's terms, so that project staff can understand the results and ask questions. For example, was the program more effective with single mothers? Did the age of the child play a role in who dropped out of the program? Were fathers and mothers equally satisfied with the program?

Instruments that provide a score allow you to quantify the degree of change after program completion. The scoring of individual instruments can usually be done by following the directions supplied with the instrument. The ease of scoring should be determined before the instrument is selected for the project. Comparing pretest and posttest scores is referred to as quantitative data analysis. Data analysis should only be done by someone with appropriate training who understands which statistical analyses are appropriate to do and how to interpret the findings.

Qualitative data analysis is a summary of process data, such as attendance, dropout rates, number of phone contacts, and participants' satisfaction. Participants and staff can also provide qualitative data by responding to open-ended questions. These data frequently provide a rich account about how a program was conducted, as well as the participants' satisfaction with it. Assessing themes in open-ended responses is, however, vulnerable to the bias of the person doing the analysis. It may be helpful to obtain an outside person, such as a graduate student, to do the qualitative analysis if an outside evaluator is not involved. (See Strauss and Corbin [1990] for a good overview of conducting qualitative data analyses and Patton [1978] for a helpful introduction to conducting evaluations in applied settings.)

# Step 5: Report and Disseminate Results

The evaluation findings should be prepared in a formal report and made available to all interested parties. Usually, the funder requires at least annual reports, even in multiyear projects. The report should be written in clear, accessible language. A suggested outline is included below.

I. Project overview and goals

II. Description of target population risk factors and needs

III. Specific objectives and activities

IV. Evaluation design and time frame

V. Project results

    A. Description of population served

    B. Implementation process

    C. Problems in implementation and adjustments

    D. Outcome and client satisfaction results

VI. Conclusions

    A. Successes, continuing challenges

    B. Future plans

    C. Implications for the field of child abuse prevention

To provide the fullest picture of the project, combine all types of data, using quotations from staff and participants and case studies along with statistical data. Although statistically significant change scores are impressive, including one or two anecdotes about particular success stories helps to put a human face on the numbers that are presented. A lengthy report should include a two- to three-page executive summary that provides a quick overview of the full-length report with key findings and conclusions highlighted. Regardless of the program's degree of success, the child abuse prevention field is in great need of reports with sound evaluation results. The program findings should be written up and submitted to professional journals.

Let us hope that as the field progresses and we develop prevention strategies with proven track records, policymakers, funders, and voters will be convinced that investing in prevention is the only prudent course. Every program's story counts as we work to make this a reality.

## References

Abidin, R. R. (1995). *Parenting stress index professional manual.* Odessa, FL: Psychological Assessment Resources, Inc.

Andrews, F. M., Klem, L., Davidson, T. N., O'Malley, P. M., & Rodgers, W. L. (1981). *A guide for selecting statistical techniques for analyzing social science data* (2nd ed.). Ann Arbor, MI: Survey Research Center Institute for Social Research, The University of Michigan.

Campbell, D. T., & Stanley, J. (1963). *Experimental & quasi-experimental designs for research.* Chicago: Rand McNally.

Cook, T., & Campbell, D. T. (1979). *Quasi-experimentation: Design & analysis for field settings.* Chicago: Rand McNally.

CSR, Inc. (1997). *Lessons learned: The experiences of nine child abuse and neglect prevention programs.* Washington, DC : Author.

Dorman, R., & Spottsville, S. (1994). *Parenting plus implementation manual.* Columbus: OH: Ohio Children's Trust Fund.

Fink, A., & Kosecoff, J. (1978). *An evaluation primer.* Newbury Park, CA: Sage Publications.

Fink, A., & McCloskey, L. (1990). Moving child abuse and neglect prevention programs forward: Improving program evaluations. *International Journal of Child Abuse and Neglect, 14* (2), 187-206.

Herman, J. L. (Ed.). (1988). *Program evaluation kit* (2nd ed.). Newbury Park, CA: Sage Publications.

Jacobs, H. F. (1988). The five-tiered approach to evaluation: Context and implementation. In H. B. Weiss & F. H. Jacobs (Eds.), *Evaluating family programs* (pp. 37-68). New York: Aldine de Gruyter.

Marshall, C., & Rossman, G. B. (1989). *Designing qualitative research.* Newbury Park, CA: Sage Publications.

Milner, J. S. (1986). *The child abuse potential inventory manual* (2nd ed.). DeKalb, IL: Psytec Inc.

Olds, D. & Kitzman, H. (1993). Review of research on home visiting for pregnant women and parents of young children. *The Future of Children, 3,* 53-92.

Olds, D. L., Eckenrode, J., Henderson, C. R., Kitzman, H., Powers, J., Cole, R., Sidora, K., Morris, P., Pettit, M. L., & Luckey, D. (1997). Long-term effects of home visitation on maternal life course and child abuse and neglect: Fifteen year follow-up of a randomized trial. *Journal of the American Medical Association, 278,* 8 (637-643).

Patton, M. Q. (1990). *Qualitative evaluation and research methods* (2nd ed.). Newbury Park, CA: Sage Publications.

Patton, M. Q. (1978). *Utilization-focused evaluation.* Beverly Hills, CA: Sage Publications.

Pietrzak, J., Ramler, M., Renner, T., Ford, L., & Gilbert, N. (1990). *Practical program evaluation: Examples from child abuse prevention.* Newbury Park: Sage Publications.

Pietrzak, J., Ramler, M., Renner, T., Ford, L., & Gilbert, N. (1990). *Practical program evaluation: Examples from child abuse prevention.* Newbury Park: Sage Publications.

Strauss, A., & Corbin, J. (1990). *Basics of qualitative research: Grounded theory procedures and techniques.* Newbury Park, CA: Sage Publications.

Touliatos, J., Perlmutter, B. F., & Straus, M. A. (Eds.). (1990). *Handbook of family measurement techniques.* Newbury Park, CA: Sage Publications.

Weiss, H. B., & Jacobs, F. H. (Eds.). (1988). *Evaluating family programs.* New York: Aldine de Gruyter.

## Resources for Evaluation Measures

Conoley, J. C., & Impara, J. C. (Eds.). (1995). *Twelfth mental measurements yearbook*. Lincoln, NE: Buros Institute of Mental Measurements.

Corcoran, K., & Fischer, J. (1994). *Measurements for clinical practice: A sourcebook* (2nd ed.). New York: The Free Press.

Johnson, O. G. (1976). *Tests and measurements in child development: Handbook II*. San Francisco: Jossey-Bass.

Lyons, J. (1997). *The measurement & management of clinical outcomes in mental health*. New York: J. Wiley.

Maruish, Mark E. (1994). *The use of psychological testing for treatment planning and outcome assessment*. Hillsdale, NJ: Erlbaum Associates.

Mitchell, J. V. (Ed.). (1983). *Tests in print III*. Highland Park, NJ: Gryphon Press.

Mullen, E. J., & Magnabosco, J. L. (1997). *Outcomes measurement in the human services: Cross-cutting issues and methods*. Washington, DC: NASW Press.

Sederer, L. I. (1996). *Outcomes assessment in clinical practice*. Baltimore: Williams & Wilkins.

Touliatos, J., Perlmutter, F. B., & Straus, A. M. (Eds.). (1990). *Handbook of family measurement techniques*. Newbury Park, CA: Sage Publications.

# Tool #1
## Structured Group Techniques

## Nominal Group

A nominal group is structured to reduce problems of group dynamics, such as domination of the group by a few higher status members. The group mixes representatives of target populations, key informants, motivated citizens, service providers, and others who are concerned with child maltreatment.

### Procedure

There should be tables for every six to nine participants, a flip pad for each table, and paper or index cards. Explain the group procedure to all the participants. Within the subgroups, include participants who represent a variety of perspectives. Present focused questions and ask the participants for several alternative solutions.

★ **Step One:** Each participant offers several answers to the first question in writing. No discussion.

★ **Step Two:** Written ideas are transferred to the flip chart in round-robin fashion. Each participant presents one idea in turn until all ideas have been listed. No discussion. (The discussion interferes with the free flow of ideas.)

★ **Step Three:** Each idea is explained and clarified. No criticism. Ideas cannot be merged. Allow approximately 25% of the time for this step.

★ **Step Four:** Each group member privately ranks the top ideas on index cards. These rankings are tallied on the flip chart.

★ **Step Five:** A brief discussion is held to clear up any misunderstandings of ideas.

★ **Step Six:** Each member again privately ranks the top ideas. Rankings from subgroups are combined for an overall tally.

Repeat the steps for each question. The result is a priority ranking of answers. The results should be compared with other findings.

# Focus Group

This technique can use members of the target population as a means of obtaining perspectives, attitudes, and beliefs regarding a problem or proposed solutions. This method is particularly helpful when program planners are not part of the target population. The interaction of the participants in a focus group provides unique viewpoints against which to compare findings from other sources. The results obtained from a focus group can validate other findings or show a need for more investigation.

## *Procedure*

★ **Step One:** Select one or two moderators to lead the discussion. The moderator should be somewhat knowledgeable about the problem and the solution being discussed.

★ **Step Two:** Select representatives of the target population. Each group consists of eight to 10 participants of equal social status. Providing an incentive to participate (gift certificate, meal, etc.) is generally helpful in securing attendance.

★ **Step Three:** Sessions generally run 60 to 90 minutes. Begin a discussion. Provide topic questions. Participants are encouraged to speak freely and contribute ideas.

The moderators help participants focus on their feelings and beliefs about the problems, issues, or solutions being discussed. Record the content of the discussion.

# Tool #2

## *Needs Assessment: Written Reports*

## Layout and Style

★ Use an attractive layout and a professional-looking cover that includes title, author(s), and logo. Separate sections with colored page breaks or tab dividers.

★ Use a clear style. Cover the topics the audience is interested in, as well as those that are necessary for decisionmaking.

## The Report Sections

### *The Executive Summary*

★ Provide overview information "at a glance."

★ Keep the length to one-and-a-half to four pages.

★ Use plain language; no jargon.

★ Simplify findings. Present the main points.

★ Present major implications of the results. (Detailed quantitative information belongs in the later report sections.)

### *Assessment Questions and Methods*

★ List the questions addressed in the report.

★ Include a short description of the methods. Mention any serious limitations and reserve the details for an appendix.

## Results

★ Summarize the results.

★ Present findings for the target population, together with expected comparison changes after receiving proposed program services. Use tables and graphs to summarize and support statements. Use qualitative information, anecdotes, interviews, or quotations to illustrate and support the quantitative statements.

## Implications

★ Show the relationship between the findings and the proposed solutions.

# Oral Presentations

An oral presentation of information adds the advantage of personal contact and allows further clarification through questions and answers. The key to oral presentation is the credibility of the speaker. Use the following format:

★ Introduce the speaker (describe qualifications and background).

★ Summarize the issues or topics covered in the presentation.

★ Briefly describe the methods used in the study.

★ Present the results of the assessment.

★ Use transparencies or slides with large typeface for key points.

★ Interpret the findings.

★ Encourage a short question-and-answer discussion.

★ Provide written copies of all overheads and slides.

# Tool #3
## Advantages and Disadvantages of Using Surveys

## Advantages of Using Surveys

★ Surveys provide a flexible means of assessing the expectations of different groups, especially when open-ended questions are used to draw out in-depth responses.

★ Surveys can be designed to address specific problems and barriers.

★ With expert help, surveys can provide causative information.

★ Surveys can be quantitative and qualitative.

★ Surveys help develop public awareness and consensus for solutions.

## Disadvantages of Using Surveys

★ Surveys frequently yield information on *wants* as opposed to actual *needs*.

★ Surveys can create expectations, in the people who take them, for immediate changes.

★ Sampling process must be done carefully to avoid biased responses.

## Other Considerations

★ Rating vs. ranking survey responses: Ranking forces the respondent to prioritize items, whereas rating permits a comparison of items along a scale. Respondents generally find rating items a simpler process than ranking, especially when there are a large number of items. Rating allows respondents to express low or high responses on any number of items. Selection of either process depends on what is wanted from the results.

★ Willingness of respondents to answer questions honestly and completely.

★ Reading level should match that of respondents.

## Advantages of Using Key Informant Surveys

★ Surveys can be designed to be quick and inexpensive.

★ Surveys are particularly valuable when the problem being investigated is rare or when the problem concerns service acceptability (maltreatment prevention program methods).

★ Surveys tap into the influence of the key informants.

★ Information and insights can be gained from individuals who have the knowledge and ability to report community needs.

## Disadvantages of Using Key Informant Surveys

★ Key informants may have biases that distort the information provided. For example, their reports may overestimate the problems or underestimate the target population's ability to cope with problems.

## Other Key Informant Survey Considerations

★ Key informants should be chosen to represent the whole range of community opinion.

★ Be sure to ask questions that are broad in range (general to specific).

# Tool #4
## Using Community Leaders as Resources

## Identifying the Right People to Contact

★ Identify actual leaders and people with influence. "Leaders" are not necessarily the same as the formal or visible people that would be expected to have influence. Community decisions are shaped by both formal and informal leaders.

★ Understand the structure of local government and identify those with formal power. Make a list of those who are immediately in contact with the geographic area where the program will be working. Build goodwill with the people you contact, especially those with regulatory power.

★ Identify "informal" community leadership by tactful questioning of established contacts. Remember that those who claim to have influence may not really have influence and are only "borrowing" influence from a less visible but real leader. Political representatives may depend on local leaders for their real influence. Be careful to observe the established rules in contacting informal leaders. Frequently, introduction or presentation of an idea by an intermediary are preferred.

★ Keep a personal notebook or file with information that may be useful as you make contacts. Keep track of names, addresses, organizations, personal interests, affiliations, or types of information that may be useful later.

★ Ask all contacts for other contact names. Add these to your note-book and look for names that are frequently mentioned. Put these persons on your list of those to be contacted.

★ Search for those who may be able to offer help in locating volun-teers, fundraising, or generating incentives or other services (i.e., food, printwork, copying, secretarial time, space for meetings, etc.) Look for support from local businesses, law practices, or those who work closely with political leaders, are on boards of banks or other large institutions or nonprofits in the community, or those who own major real estate holdings (e.g., VIPs, politicians, reli-gious leaders, businessmen/women, school board members, etc.).

★ Call agencies or organizations and ask for the names of people who head departments or are appointed to positions with influ-ence.

★ Look at past issues that are related to your program area and find out who supported or opposed them. Informal community lead-ers are more likely to play a role in issues they consider to be of greater importance. Identify the informal leaders who take an in-terest in family and children's issues.

★ Join organizations, volunteer to be on committees, and attend seminars or workshops to meet with experienced individuals from the community or those who have accurate firsthand knowledge about the community. Find out which persons are on planning councils or other coordinating meetings. Become acquainted with the range of viewpoints in the community.

## How Are the Right People Contacted?

★ Ask someone you know to introduce you to the person. Use mem-bers of advisory boards, panels, or other citizen or professional organizations for introductions. Just getting in to see someone with "influence" is not as effective as seeing them in a carefully chosen situation or through persons they respect.

★ Attend meetings, functions, or other gatherings where the person(s) you wish to meet are also attending. Remember, people will support and advocate activities that they "invest" in financially or emotionally. These groups or boards are good areas from which to get initial feedback for testing a program idea or to gauge acceptance or support for an idea.

★ Invitations to join organizations or groups depends on becoming visible. Be present where members meet (e.g., school or civic functions, ground breakings, open houses, speakers forums, health fairs, etc.). If the program idea is already developed, display a poster or make a simple leaflet available by way of introducing the idea.

★ Write a letter of introduction and follow it up with a brief phone call. Ask for some time to speak with the person at a later time. Set up a time to meet.

★ Use a newsletter or flyer concerning something related to the project idea with a personal note indicating that the person contacted would want to know about the information. Limit the content of such messages to what the contact person would find relevant. Avoid pressing a personal viewpoint. Instead, recognize the contact person's past efforts, involvement with, or interest in the topic. If a response is received, listen and be attentive to viewpoints, positive remarks, or signs of interest in pursuing the idea. Ask to meet personally with the person at some convenient time.

★ Let your contacts know that the purpose of the initial contact is to become familiar with those persons who have special knowledge about the community. Ask them for their ideas based on the particular expertise that they have. Maintain a receptive attitude and absorb all the information that is offered, whether it seems relevant or not. Limit the initial contact to topics and issues that are relevant to the person contacted. If the person contacted potentially has more information to offer, arrange a second meeting.

## Awareness Factors

★ Informal community leaders or others who live within or work closely with the community population are especially valuable sources of information when statistics are unavailable or when a qualitative viewpoint can clarify statistics.

★ In making contact with ethnic or cultural minority leaders, use the same approaches. Be aware that ethnic or cultural minorities are not always represented proportionately in the formal power structure. There may be, however, a hierarchy of leadership within that cultural community.

★ Maintain cultural awareness. Be alert to cultural clues and respect cultural patterns and forms of communication and process.

★ Look for common beliefs in the community. These will help identify "major" issue areas. Associating "new" activities, such as a prevention program, to these dominant views allows for transference of support by the community members.

★ "Major" community leaders tend to be interested and involved in what they perceive as "major" community matters, especially in prioritizing their own investment of time and energy. Sometimes, emerging leaders are more willing to devote their time to a program if they see a mutual benefit in becoming associated with the program.

★ Develop "political savvy" about the community power structure. Becoming acquainted with people with influence will help you establish allies throughout the project.

It is important to establish a working relationship with as many community leaders as possible. Ask present contacts for referrals to other persons who can provide insights and information and advice. A project can never have too many supporters. Advocacy from several sources is the best way to achieve support and ensure program success.

## References

Corrick, G. W., & Detweiler, J. S. (1980). Involving community leadership and citizens. In T. D. Conners (Ed.), *The nonprofit organization handbook*, pp. 5-23. New York: McGraw-Hill.

# Tool #5
## Developing Objectives and Clear Statements of Need

## Developing Objectives

Program objectives should be carefully constructed, worded to avoid misinterpretation, and relate the following information:

★ Who or what the target is (include numbers)

★ What is going to change, be modified, improve, decrease, etc.

★ How much change is expected (measured by test, observation, self-report, finished product, etc.)

★ When changes (e.g., behavior, attitudes, etc.) or products (e.g., materials such as curricula, posters, etc.) are to be accomplished (provide timelines)

★ Means of accomplishment (e.g., instruction, practice, discussion, role play, develop, design, etc.)

## Developing Clear Statements and Descriptions

Using accurate wording to describe a need addressed by a prevention project enables others to clearly see the need and the solutions proposed by the project, as well as to see the connection between them.

The components of a good description of need include a "cause," a subsequent "effect" or "need," the "symptoms" of the condition, and the "target" of the action. These descriptive elements are useful for

**167**

describing the problem or need uncovered by the needs assessment. Frequently, a short, concise (sometimes one sentence) description of a project is required by funders or for public relations pieces or for other purposes.

## The Elements to Include in a Program Description

★ Type of prevention (primary, secondary, tertiary)

★ Focus of prevention (research, education, public awareness, etc.)

★ Purpose of prevention (reduction of a form of abuse, improve an existing program, etc.)

Following are some examples of program description statements and need statements using excerpts from the program narrative of the Parenting Plus Project, Cuyahoga County, Ohio.

**Program Description:** The Parenting Plus Project is a secondary prevention research/demonstration project designed to test the efficacy of parenting skills training alone or in combination with social support in preventing physical abuse and neglect.

**Statement of Need:**

★ **Cause:** "...few programs have attempted an integrated approach combining the emotional support of a one-to-one relationship and a parent training component to determine whether such a combined approach will be more successful than either component itself..."

★ **Effect:** "...a 1985 report by the Head Start Synthesis Project...reviewed all relevant research and concluded that: 'The impact of Head Start on parental childrearing practices has been mixed...it is clear that a stronger impact on parent-child relationships can only be achieved by more intensive efforts...'"

★ **Symptom:** "For a demonstration project to be truly successful, it must effectively prevent abuse and be easily transferable to other sites. Many demonstration projects have never been replicated because of the cost and effort of setting up the program...(due to the fact that they do not) utilize existing community structures (such as Head Start and Retired Senior Volunteer Programs) as a foundation for the project."

★ **Target:** "One hundred and twenty Head Start parents will be selected for inclusion in the project by Head Start personnel. Most Head Start parents live below the poverty line and therefore are deemed high risk for abuse and neglect...Head Start is a logical program to serve as the...foundation, since it serves a high risk population, is located across the state and nation, and has parent involvement as a key part of the program..."

# Tool #6
## Working with Volunteers

The creative use of volunteers is a means of enhancing the service delivery for prevention projects. The effective use of volunteers depends on understanding the motivations, needs, and interests of each volunteer and matching them to an appropriate support service within the project.

Should volunteers be used? For any project, this decision should be made in the project designing stage based on an assessment of the appropriateness of utilizing volunteers and on the availability of volunteers who have the necessary skills required by the project. Once it has been decided to incorporate volunteers into the project, it is necessary to look at recruitment, training, and retention of volunteers as a part of implementation.

## Recruitment

Volunteers do a job, and in most respects, they should be treated the same as a paid staff person. The "position" volunteers will be filling should be well described, with qualifications and skills as well as responsibilities and time commitments clearly outlined.

The activities the volunteers will perform help in deciding where recruitment activities should begin. For instance, if particular skills are required (e.g., photography, organizing, clerical, etc.), then special interest groups, hobby clubs and service organizations, or businesses using those skills would be logical places to look for volunteers.

Make contact with potential volunteers using several media and network contacts. In flyers, news ads, posters, or other media messages, provide some information about the volunteer activity, the goals of the project, and the kind of person or skills wanted, as well as the amount of time commitment and potential benefits for the volunteer (e.g., experience, opportunities to meet new people, or develop new skills, etc.). Be sure to include a contact person's name, telephone number, and address on any of these messages.

## Why Do People Volunteer?

The key to finding volunteers is to identify the motivation factors for each candidate. Most people volunteer for reasons similar to the following:

★ To learn new skills and for self-improvement

★ To increase social interaction

★ For recognition and to prove self-worth

★ To have an opportunity to share personal ideas, opinions, or problems with others

★ To satisfy a sense of responsibility or to contribute as a means of repaying society

★ Because of a personal empathy with the program goals or the target population

★ To be useful or influential

Don't limit recruitment to traditional sources, such as homemakers, church group members, college students, etc. Consider looking for recruits among nontraditional groups: nonjoiners or unaffiliated persons, men, minority groups, persons lacking formal education, persons in rural areas, the young, persons with physical or mental disabilities, the retired, and business professionals. Ask program participants or other volunteers to suggest potential volunteers.

The potential volunteer's perception of the project greatly influences his or her decision to contribute time and talent; therefore, it is important to make positive impressions, especially on first contact.

★ Always speak to a potential volunteer personally. If the first contact is by phone, follow up with a handwritten note and a brochure or other information about the project.

★ Set up an interview at a time and location convenient for the volunteer.

★ After initial contact, invite potential volunteers to visit the office or a presentation, if that is appropriate.

## Effective Interviewing

Important insights are revealed in the interview, if the right questions are asked. Other qualities besides educational background or experience may be required, such as cultural awareness or an unbiased attitude or an ability to empathize.

The interview is also an opportunity to let the prospective volunteer know that particular skills or talents are valued. The following steps will guide the interviewer in arriving at an accurate assessment:

★ Interview the volunteer applicant in a friendly, private setting.

★ Have the volunteer fill out an application form. The form should be similar to an employment form with added emphasis on interests, hobbies, and reasons for seeking the volunteer position.

★ Clarify the purpose of the interview. Ask if the prospective volunteer understood the literature or the goals of the project.

★ Ask open-ended questions: What former volunteer experience did you enjoy most? What was most satisfying? What types of people do you enjoy working with? (or not enjoy working with?) What do you think would be your greatest contribution to this volunteer program? Include questions of a specific nature if specific qualities are required (e.g., other language fluency, reactions to project, similar situations, etc.).

★ Go over the commitment requirements of the position: hours, days, flexibility. Be sure that these will be satisfactory.

★ Let the applicant ask questions. Listen carefully to determine where her/his concerns or interests fall.

★ Most projects will require volunteers with specific skills or expertise that match the program design. If a volunteer does not fit the needs of the project say so, but offer to put the volunteer in contact with another project or agency that could use the person's abilities.

★ Immediately after the interview, take time to make notes about impressions, questions, or any follow-up information that is needed.

### "Hiring" the Volunteer

Just as with regular staff, select volunteers with skills and an interest in doing the work that match the needs of the project. Offer the position to the person and explain any contingencies. Complete the necessary paperwork, especially the background check, to reveal whether there is any previous connection to maltreatment reports, and check their references.

### Orientation

Volunteers should receive an orientation that includes an overview and/or history of the project, the role and rights/responsibilities of the volunteer(s), and policies and procedures (e.g., reimbursements, training, reporting, use of equipment, etc.). Make these available in a notebook.

## Training

Together with the volunteer(s), plan out a training sequence that will prepare the volunteer to perform assigned tasks. Set learning objectives regarding information level, skill level, and behavior and attitudes, etc. Make a calendar of training experiences (in-agency or away) for the volunteer to attend, as well as some form of evaluation to measure mastery of skills, etc.

### Managing Volunteers

Effective management will help retain volunteers. Volunteer satisfaction depends on having adequate direction, support, and feedback so that they are enabled to do their best work.

★ Clearly define job responsibilities and make sure that the volunteer understands them.

★ Show trust by not checking work too frequently; however, maintain enough contact to show interest and provide feedback and support.

★ Include volunteers in decisionmaking by asking for feedback, suggestions, and other input.

★ Establish performance standards and provide regular feedback in the form of constructive appraisals. Acknowledge accomplishments personally and publicly in newsletters, on bulletin boards, or at meetings.

★ Be a positive listener. Offer direction that builds on strengths.

★ Set and maintain record-keeping procedures for hours, activities, training, etc.

## Retention

Retaining volunteers is a critical factor for most projects because of the short-term nature of the funding arrangement and the investment of time and effort in training good volunteers.

The attitude of the project staff towards volunteers is a primary influence on volunteer performance and retention. The staff must be prepared to work with volunteers and become comfortable with the role of the volunteer in the project so as not to harbor resentments or insecurities due to unclear perceptions. Include project staff in decisions about where and how to use volunteers and in designing job descriptions. Recognize staff who work well with volunteers.

Volunteers should be assigned to meaningful jobs that satisfy their reasons for volunteering. Volunteers acquire a sense of value when they are included in training, get recognition and are asked to contribute input or opinions. Reward competence with greater responsibility.

Scheduled progress report or evaluations are good opportunities to find out how satisfied the volunteer is and to work out any negative feelings. Good communication about project goals and the role the volunteer plays in achieving them fosters growth and satisfaction.

## Recognition

The volunteer's paycheck is recognition. Either formal or informal expressions of appreciation validate the volunteer experience. Recognition and appreciation should be courteous, respectful, genuine, and in line with the actual contribution.

### Formal Recognition

★ A year-end program, ceremony, or luncheon

★ A letter or certificate of appreciation

★ Special plaques, pins, or other visible objects

### Informal Recognition

★ Daily courtesies (coffee breaks, birthday cards, etc.)

★ Timely reimbursement for parking, meals, transportation, etc.

★ Records of volunteer hours or personal recommendations to use as references

*Other Forms of Recognition*

★ Titles, advancement, opportunities to train new volunteers

★ Assignment to valued tasks or activities

★ News interview or photo session

★ Tokens, gifts, etc.

## Resources

Conners, T. D. (Ed.). (1980). *The nonprofit organization handbook*. New York: McGraw-Hill.

Minnesota Office on Volunteer Services. (1984). *Volunteer for Minnesota: Community handbook, Part 2*. Available from Minnesota Office on Volunteer Services, Department of Administration, 500 Rice Street, St. Paul, MN 55155.

National Information Center on Volunteerism. (1985). *Partnership and volunteerism: Effective utilization of community involvement*. Presented at 19th National Migrant Education Conference in Atlanta, Georgia. Available from National Information Center on Volunteerism, P.O. Box 4179, Boulder, CO 80306.

# Tool #7
## Training

Any training planned by a prevention project should aim at directly improving the ability of the project staff to reach program goals and objectives. This is accomplished in the following ways:

★ Selecting training topics and content that have a direct bearing on staff performance

★ Gearing training content to the level of the staff being trained; this may mean different trainings for different staff

★ Selecting a trainer with expertise, skill in training, and the ability to adapt the content to the needs of the project

## Topics

Certain topics should be covered as part of the training for every project:

★ Project policies and procedures

★ The maltreatment law and reporting procedures

★ Maltreatment indicators

★ Dealing with work-related stresses

★ Special issues related to each project, such as cultural differences, physical differences (disabled population), or language differences.

In addition, projects using skills in such areas as administering tests, interviewing, or completing progress forms or other data records may need to cover these in training sessions.

The level and type of expertise that the project staff have will dictate which training topics are necessary. For instance, some staff may have advanced degrees in counseling or therapy but little training in delivering this service in a culturally sensitive and competent manner. On the other hand, project volunteers may be much in tune with the cultural attitudes and perspectives of the target population, but lack professional training in counseling. In this instance, a training with three components, one dealing with fundamental counseling skills for the volunteers, one addressing cultural sensitivity issues for the staff, and one with a practice session using staff and volunteers in role-playing situations, could raise the level of competence of everyone.

## The Trainer

Every trainer must have expertise and the ability to help others learn that expertise. To find a competent trainer, interview prospective trainers and check references. Find out if he/she will adapt the training to the specific needs of the project.

Trainers can come from within the project or parent agency or an outside agency. To locate trainers outside an agency, check with contacts at local child protection agencies and health care, education and judiciary systems, and organizations devoted to reducing child maltreatment.

## Training Format

All training sessions should use a variety of activities. In general, training should move from introductory information and concepts to specific knowledge and skills that are applicable to the project. Newly learned or adapted skills are retained better if they are reinforced through simulation or practice. Using several methods of presentation (e.g., lecture, audiovisual aides, demonstration, etc.) also increases retention.

The most effective training occurs in smaller groups (five to nine persons). When larger groups are necessary, the addition of question-

and-answer discussions, and/or time to work in subgroups on assigned activities, is a good method of reinforcing lecture material.

## General Guidelines

★ Limit lectures to 20 minutes in length, or 40 minutes with several changes in pace or activity.

★ Limit discussions and exercises to 40 minutes or less.

★ Films should always be accompanied by a discussion.

★ Allow enough time for "hands-on" activities. It may take some time for people to warm up to an activity and then really process it.

★ Plan a break for any session lasting more than two hours.

★ Plan ahead to have seating arrangements, equipment, or other materials ready. Make sure the physical environment is comfortable (room temperature, air circulation, lighting, etc.)

# Training Techniques

Select a technique that best suits the material being presented and the knowledge and skill of the trainers and participants.

## Lecture

Lectures are a good method of presenting a great deal of information in a short period of time and of introducing ideas or concepts.

★ State the purpose of the lecture first.

★ Cover only two or three key learning points.

★ Limit to 20 minutes, pace variation, or use other technique.

## Panel

A panel brings together three to six persons with different points of view to discuss or debate a topic. It provides a stimulating diversity of perspectives and expertise, but does not allow much audience involvement.

★ Limit panelist presentations or "floor time" to a few minutes.

★ Structure the format to alternate viewpoints with rebuttals.

★ Add a question-and-answer period at the end.

## Brainstorming

Brainstorming creates lists of a group's ideas on one subject at a time. Use from 3 to 12 people.

★ Write the topic or subject on a chalkboard or flipchart.

★ List all ideas that are called out by participants, without editing or questioning.

★ Review and comment, then summarize.

## Role Playing

Role playing is an effective means of acting out problems and approaches to solutions. It is an effective practice method and is an excellent way of demonstrating complex attitudes and skills. Role reversal switches roles and helps participants to see other patterns of reaction or interaction, increases sensitivity to other points of view, and demonstrates a variety of perspectives.

★ Assign roles and limit time.

## Guided Group Discussion

This technique facilitates process learning and observation skills, and can be used to cover large topics more efficiently by assigning portions to different groups.

★ A group representing a variety of backgrounds can problem solve different questions drawing on their combined expertise.

★ A group is divided so that half of the group actively discuss a topic, while the other half observes the process.

★ A broad topic can be covered by assigning portions to different groups. The groups report and share their conclusions.

# Evaluate the Training

Evaluate every training. Design questions so they can be easily rated on a scale. Include some open-ended questions to get a range of feedback. Keep the evaluation short and easy to complete.

## Evaluation Questions

★ Were the goals of the training session clear? Were they met?

★ What was the effectiveness of the trainer?

★ Are there other questions, comments, recommendations?

★ What was liked most/least?

★ What is overall rating for session?

## Contingencies

Prevention-related trainings may cover sensitive topics. Be prepared for some possible reactions.

★ There may be persons present who may have been abused, were abusers, or know abusers. Reactions may be defensive or hostile, or extreme sensitivity may be expressed. Be prepared for disclosures and have a list of community services available to make referrals.

★ Turf disputes and related "political" or issue-related disputes may be triggered by some topics.

★ Disagreements over viewpoints or methods may require some diplomatic management.

Use appropriate humor as a way of dealing with serious subject matter and strong emotions.

## Resources

Government agencies and prevention-oriented organizations, as well as educational institutions, have libraries of audiovisual materials that are available at no cost or for reasonable rental fees. Contact them for a catalog of resources or resource directories. (See Appendixes B and C for national resources.)

Check for free or low-cost training made available through state or local programs. (See list below.)

★ Children's Trust Fund

★ Mental health centers

★ Public health agencies

★ Professional organizations

★ Boards of education

★ Speakers Bureaus from community organizations and industry

★ Child protection services

★ National Committee for Prevention of Child Abuse local chapter

# Tool #8
## Public Relations Tools for Prevention Projects

## Fact Sheet

It is a good idea for a project to prepare a general "fact sheet" that covers the main items of information about the project. Use the fact sheet as a part of the initial contact with the general public, other agency personnel, political contacts, other professionals in education or health fields, as handouts, etc. The fact sheet should contain the following information:

★ The name, address, telephone number (including any crisis number), and the purpose of the organization, stated in simple language.

★ A few statements (one or two paragraphs) about the beginning date, the population being served and numbers, the principal source of funding, names of key project staff, and the name and telephone number of a person responsible for media contact, program registration, speaking arrangements, etc.

★ Include a few remarks about successful accomplishments or other interesting information, such as sponsored events.

## The Media

The media include newspapers (local and ethnic); radio; television; magazines; placards on buses; printed materials (leaflets, brochures, posters, direct mail, advertising, billboards); speakers; and other specialized media, such as professional journals, business newsletters, or club and association publications.

Every project should be familiar with the basic guidelines of working with media:

★ Start with lists of newspapers, stations, persons, etc.

★ Find out who the contact person is.

★ Start with a *short* personal visit or phone call with the contact person. Find out the preferred procedure for using the media, such as deadlines, format, word limits, best times to call, etc. Hand deliver a fact sheet and make personal contact.

★ Mail or hand deliver news or promotional information.

★ In dealing with news media contacts come to the point quickly, be honest, and don't give incorrect information. Keep contact to a minimum; contact only when there is something worthwhile to convey. Don't be disappointed if the news item is not printed or aired.

★ Do not reveal information that is confidential.

## Written Materials for News Media

★ Communicate clearly and concisely. Keep the content to the point, maintain consistency in statements, and consider the comprehension level of the audience.

★ News releases stick to the reporter's fundamental 5 Ws: who, what, when, where, and why. Add only important details and remember that editors cut stories. Write a headline that tells the editor what the article is about.

★ Feature stories are meant to interpret, instruct, or entertain. Present facts in an interesting and friendly manner. For topics, use accomplishments of your project or particular participants, staff members, or volunteers. Contact the editor about the story idea before writing it.

★ Letters to the editor can be an excellent way to present project information. Keep them short and positive in tone. If the letter is a rebuttal, send it within one week of the appearance of the original article or letter in the news media.

## Other Media Contacts

★ Photographs are good supplements for feature stories. Keep a file with photographs of *active positive activities* that occur as part of the project. These may be used in a variety of situations. Use 35-mm, black-and-white film, and professional processing if pictures are intended to be reproduced in print. Always provide a caption on a piece of paper and attach the picture to it. Persons in the photograph should sign a release for using it.

★ News conferences are only called when a serious event or issue has aroused public interest concern or curiosity. This situation may require considerable expertise to handle professionally. Get advice before agreeing to one.

## Broadcast Media

★ Provide a good story, volunteer for talk shows, submit public service announcements, or buy advertising time.

★ Public affairs segments are always looking for good program ideas. This is excellent, free coverage. Suggest a possible format.

★ Public service announcements (PSAs) are usually reserved for local interests. There is much competition for these spots, so the most professional-looking PSAs have an edge. Spots run for 10, 20, or 30 seconds. For these spots, a short prevention message (5-15 words), followed by information on how to contact the project, is about all that can be presented. Preparing television spots requires professional advice. Ask for help from the media department of a local college, university, or media school.

★ Coverage of an event requires notifying media several days prior to that event. Provide time, date, location, and event description. Mention who may be interested in and may benefit from attending or participating.

★ Make an announcement that is eye catching and provide a noticeable headline.

## Promotional Project Materials

★ A **leaflet** can convey basic information about the project and services. It is extremely useful as a giveaway. It resembles the fact sheet, with extra information and formatting. Be sure it fits a standard envelope. It can be printed inexpensively on a high-quality copier with better quality paper stock.

★ **Brochures or pamphlets** are more expensive to produce and should only be considered if long-term funding is approved. Use a professional printer and get several estimates. Remember, do not tell everything about the program in the brochure.

★ **Posters** are limited-use items. Be sure the project can really benefit from the investment. If the poster does not have to be professional quality, look into making one using high-quality materials.

★ **Direct mail** can be expensive, depending on the numbers on the mailing list. However, this is a good method of reaching key persons with updates. Extensive mailings can be done if high-tech printing, sorting, and addressing equipment or computer programs are available.

★ **Advertising**, in special circumstances, is the only way to reach a mass audience and maintain total control of the message content. It is expensive and you should obtain expert advice. There is some free print space available. Check with advertising companies or try local schools with media programs for assistance.

★ **Speakers Bureaus** are a highly effective means of reaching the public or particular audiences. Make sure speakers are effective, materials are factual and interesting, and one person does the scheduling. If possible, find qualified volunteers to train for this. They are excellent representatives.

★ Join **community and professional groups**. This is one way to meet the most influential and concerned people and exchange ideas informally.

★ Maltreatment events typically stir public interest. This may be a good time to advertise your project. Present information, advocate, and suggest solutions.

## Resources

Conners, T. D. (Ed.). (1980). *The nonprofit organization handbook*. New York: McGraw-Hill.

U.S. Department of Health, Education, and Welfare. (1980, June). *How to plan and carry out a successful public awareness program on child abuse and neglect*. [DHHS Publication No. (OHDS) 80-30089]. Washington, DC: U.S. Government Printing Office.

# *Appendix A*
## *Abuse Indicators**

There are many general characteristics shown by parents and children which may indicate that some form of maltreatment is taking place. It is always important, however, to remember that these indicators can be signs of other stressors and may exist even if the child is *not* being maltreated. Different families respond to stress in different ways. These indicators could be signs of abuse and neglect *or* signs that something else is causing difficulties for the child.

*Don't* ignore these signs. Be aware of what they might indicate, and if you suspect maltreatment is causing the behavior or physical sign, report your suspicions to the Department of Human Services according to your agency or project policy. (See Appendix F for a model reporting form.)

Prevention project professionals need to be aware of the following:

★ The "model" child who is *too* well-behaved may be indicating something by this **overly compliant or too-mature behavior**.

★ **Any change in behavior** from the child's norm (suddenly becoming fearful or aggressive) may be an indication of maltreatment.

---

\* **Source:** Mitchell, J. L. (1990). Recognizing maltreatment. *In* Knell, S. M., Dorman, R. L., McMillin, K., & Mitchell, J. L. (1990). *Child abuse recognition and prevention resource and reference manual*. Columbus, OH: Ohio Children's Trust Fund.

★ Every child is an individual, and therefore **every child may react differently to maltreatment situations.**

Parents who display the following characteristics or living situations may be more likely to maltreat their child in some way:

★ Difficulty dealing with aggressive impulses/controlling anger

★ Tendency to be rigid and domineering

★ Lacks knowledge regarding child development (has unrealistic expectations of what the child is capable of doing)

★ Substance (alcohol/drug) abuse

★ Difficulty dealing with stress

★ Emotionally immature

★ Lacks emotional attachment to the child

★ Mental illness

The following lists are to be used as guides for recognizing physical abuse, sexual abuse, emotional abuse, and physical neglect. **This does not** mean that *all* signs of maltreatment are listed here—you may know some indicators that are *not* listed here. These lists are meant to be used as *basic guidelines* and should be used in combination with your own good judgment.

The first column shows some of the physical signs the child may show that might indicate abuse or neglect. The second column lists some of the behaviors the child may display that are also an indication of maltreatment. The third column lists some of the typical characteristics of the parent who is maltreating her child.

## Physical Abuse

### Physical Indicators

Unexplained bruises or welts
- On several different areas of the body
- In cluster or unusual patterns
- In the shape of the instrument used to inflict them

Unexplained burns
- In the shape of the instrument used to inflict them (cigarette, rope, iron)
- Caused by immersion in hot liquid (burn may be glovelike or socklike in appearance

Unexplained lacerations or abrasions
- To lip and mouth area
- To external genitalia
- On backs of arms, legs, torso

Unexplained skeletal injuries
- Fractures of skull or face
- Multiple fractures
- Stiff, swollen joints
- Bald spots from pulling hair
- Missing or loosened teeth
- Human-sized bite marks (especially if adult-sized and recurrent)
- Detached retina (from shaking or hitting)

School absence at the time of appearance of injury

Clothing is inappropriate for the weather
- Long-sleeved shirt in summer to cover bruises

### Child's Behavior

Extremes in behavior
- Very aggressive
- Very withdrawn
- Submissive, overly compliant—caters to adults
- Hyperactive
- Depressed/apathetic

Easily fearful or frightened
- Of parents, adults
- Of physical contact
- Of going home
- When other children cry

Destructive to self and others

Poor social relations
- Craves affection
- Indiscriminate attachment to strangers
- Relates poorly to peers
- Manipulates adults to get attention

Reports
- Fear of parent(s)
- Injuries inflicted by parent
- Unbelievable reasons for injuries (to protect parents)

Demonstrates poor self-concept

Learning problems
- Poor academic performance
- Short attention span
- Language delayed

Chronic runaway

Delinquency

### Parental Characteristics

Conceals the child's injury
- Gives explanation that doesn't fit the injury or has no explanation
- Dresses the child to cover the injury
- Keeps child home from school

Does not appeared concerned about the child
- Cares more about what will happen to him/her than what will happen to the child
- Describes the child as bad, evil, or different

Believes in severe or inappropriate discipline for child's age and size

Unrealistic expectations
- Regarding development
- Regarding emotional gratification (expects child to fill emotional void)

Low self-esteem

Abuses alcohol and/or drugs

Immature

Maltreated as child

## *Sexual Abuse*

### Physical Indicators

Difficulty walking

Torn, stained, bloody underclothing

Abnormalities in genital/anal areas
- Itching, pain, swelling
- Bruising or bleeding
- Frequent urinary or yeast infections
- Vaginal/penal discharge
- Poor sphincter control

Venereal disease

Pregnancy

Psychosomatic illness

### Child's Behavior

Sudden drop in school performance

Poor peer relationships

Unwillingness to change clothing for gym

Sexual knowledge beyond age
- Displays bizarre or sophisticated sexual behavior
- Seductive behavior
- Excessive masturbation

Poor self-concept
- Depressed/apathetic
- Suicidal

Extremes in behavior
- Sexually aggressive
- Withdrawn/fearful of males

Regression to earlier developmental stage
- Withdrawn
- Engages in fantasy or babylike behaviors

Chronic runaway

Delinquency

### Parental Characteristics

Possessive and jealous of victim
- Denies the child normal social contact
- Accuses child or sexual promiscuity and seductiveness

Low self-esteem

Poor impulse control

Was sexually abused as a child

Abuses alcohol and/or drugs

Socially isolated

Poor relationship with spouse

Believes child enjoys sexual contact

Believes sexual contact expresses family love

## *Emotional Maltreatment*

### Child's Behavior

Learning problems

Developmental lags
- Physical, emotional, intellectual

Extremes in behavior
- Aggressive
- Withdrawn

Destructive to self and others

Sleep disorders

Demonstrates poor self-concept
- Depressed/apathetic
- Suicidal

Problems in day care/school
- Developmental delays or hyper-activity

Problems in dealing with new situations or people
- Overly anxious
- Pseudo-maturity

Fearful, lacking in creativity

### Parental Characteristics

Unrealistic expectations of child

Belittles, rejects, degrades, ignores the child

Threatens child
- With severe punishment
- With abandonment

Describes the child as bad, different, evil

Low self-esteem

Does not seem to care about the child's problems

## *Physical Neglect*

| Physical Indicators | Child's Behavior | Parental Characteristics |
|---|---|---|
| Poor growth pattern | Developmental lags | Apathetic/passive |
| - Emaciated | - Physical, emotional, intellectual | Depressed |
| - Distended stomach | Extremes in behavior | Unconcerned with child |
| Consistent hunger/ malnutrition | - Hyperactive | - Is not bothered by child's lack of basic necessities nor by child's behavior due to his/her negligence |
| Poor hygiene | - Aggressive | |
| - Lice | - Withdrawn | |
| - Body odor | - Assumes adult responsibilities | |
| Lacks appropriate, necessary clothing | - Acts in a pseudo-mature fashion | - Does not seek child care |
| Unattended physical problems or medical needs | - Submissive/overly compliant | - No food in house |
| - Lack of proper immunization | Infantile behavior | Socially isolated |
| | Depressed/apathetic | Low self-esteem |
| - Gross dental problems | - States that no one cares | Abuses alcohol and/or drugs |
| - Needs glasses/ hearing aids | Begs/steals food | Impulsive |
| Constant lack of supervision | - Forages through garbage | Mentally retarded |
| | - Consistent hunger | Maltreated as child |
| - Especially in dangerous activities or circumstances | Seeks affection/attention | Unsafe living conditions |
| | - Hypochondria | - Chaotic home life, overcrowding |
| Constant fatigue/listlessness | Consistent absence or tardiness at school | - Drugs/poisons in reach of children |
| - Falls asleep in school | Delinquency | - Garbage and/or excrement in living area |

# Appendix B
## Federal Resources for
## Child Abuse and Neglect
## Prevention Activities

The Interagency Task Force on Child Abuse and Neglect, a group of 30 federal agencies, was established in 1988 through an amendment to the Child Abuse Prevention and Treatment Act (CAPTA) to coordinate efforts to reduce child maltreatment throughout the United States. Several member agencies conduct activities that support prevention activities. Federal agencies typically award funding to states and/or individual programs and institutions through a Request for Proposal (RFP) process. Announcements for available funds are published in the *Federal Register*.

### U.S. Department of Health and Human Services
*http://www.dhhs.gov*
The Department of Health and Human Services has several agencies that provide support for child abuse and neglect prevention activities:
- Children's Bureau/National Center on Child Abuse and Neglect
- Head Start Bureau
- Administration on Developmental Disabilities
- Public Health Service

### Children's Bureau/National Center on Child Abuse and Neglect (NCCAN)
P.O. Box 1182
Washington, DC 20013
*http://www.acf.dhhs.gov/programs/cb*

The Children's Bureau/NCCAN is the lead source of funding for child abuse and neglect activities within the federal government. This agency allocates funds to states for prevention activities as well as to community-based prevention organizations.

The community-based Family Resource and Support Program is a formula grant program for states to establish and coordinate a comprehensive network of family resource and support services. Discretionary grants can be obtained by community-based programs to establish, maintain, and evaluate child abuse and neglect prevention activities.

### Head Start Bureau
P.O. Box 1182
Washington, DC 20013
*http://www.acf.dhhs.gov/programs/hsb*

This agency administers a national program for preschool children and their families. Activities related to child maltreatment include staff training on child abuse and neglect identification and reporting, public awareness and education, and parental involvement.

### Administration on Developmental Disabilities
Hubert H. Humphrey Building
200 Independence Avenue, SW
Washington, DC 20201
*http://www.acf.dhhs.gov/programs/add*

The Administration on Developmental Disabilities provides support to enable people with developmental disabilities to achieve their maximum potential. Formula and discretionary grants are available through this agency. Discretionary grants may support child abuse and neglect prevention activities through early intervention services, program models, and protection of legal and human rights.

### Public Health Service
Parklawn Building
5600 Fishers Lane
Rockville, MD 20857

The Public Health Service is involved in activities related to child abuse and neglect through several agencies:
- Centers for Disease Control and Prevention, National Center for Injury Prevention and Control
  *http://www.cdc.gov/ncipc/dvp/dvp.htm*
- Indian Health Service
  *http://www.tucson.ihs.gov*
- Office of Disease Prevention and Health Promotion

## U.S. Department of Education
600 Maryland Avenue, SW
Washington, DC 20202
*http://www.ed.gov*

Within the U.S. Department of Education, the Office of Elementary and Secondary Education and the Office of Special Education and Rehabilitation Services engage in activities related to child maltreatment.

## Office of Elementary and Secondary Education
400 Maryland Avenue, SW
Washington, DC 20202-6100
*http://www.ed.gov/offices/OESE*

This office carries out child abuse and neglect prevention, public awareness/education, and demonstration project activities through four program offices:
- Compensatory Education Programs
  *http://www.ed.gov/offices/OESE/CEP/*
- Office of Indian Education
  *http://www.ed.gov/offices/OESE/indian.html*
- Office of Migrant Education
  *http://www.ed.gov/offices/OESE/mep.html*
- School Improvement Programs
  *http://www.ed.gov/offices/OESE/sip.html*

## Office of Special Education and Rehabilitation Services
Mary Switzer Building
330 C Street, SW
Washington, DC 20202-2500
*http://www.ed.gov/offices/OSERS*

This office provides formula grants to states and other organizations to improve educational outcomes for children and adults with disabilities, including abused and neglected children. Emphasis is on special education programs, early intervention, resource development, and service delivery improvement.

### U.S. Department of Justice
*http://www.usdoj.gov*

The Department of Justice supports activities related to child maltreatment prevention by collecting crime statistics (Bureau of Justice Statistics), supporting training in the prosecution of child abuse cases (Bureau of Justice Assistance), and training law enforcement personnel (Federal Bureau of Investigation). The Office of Juvenile Justice and Delinquency Prevention supports prevention activities.

### Office of Juvenile Justice and Delinquency Prevention
633 Indiana Avenue, NW
Washington, DC 20531
*http://ncjrs.org/ojjhome.htm*

Recognizing the link between maltreatment and subsequent juvenile delinquency, OJJDP recently initiated demonstration projects to reduce child abuse and neglect in several communities (Safe Kids/Safe Streets). Other activities include training and technical assistance to states, discretionary grants to organizations to support delinquency prevention, and support for professionals working with juvenile victims and offenders.

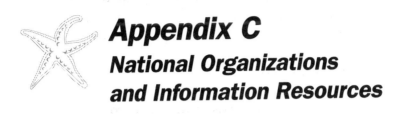

# Appendix C
## National Organizations
## and Information Resources

These organizations and sources are offered as suggestions for where to locate additional assistance and information. They focus on child abuse prevention and/or family support activities.

## National Organizations

### The ABA Center on Children and the Law
740 15th Street, NW
Washington, DC 20005
202/662-1000
*http://www.abanet.org/child*

A program of the American Bar Association, Young Lawyers Division. The Center's objectives are to increase professional awareness and competency of the legal community in the area of child welfare issues. Develops publications relating to child abuse and neglect, sexual abuse, permanency planning, child custody, foster care, and child and family development.

### American Humane Association, Children's Division
63 Inverness Drive East
Englewood, CO 80112-5117
303/792-9900  Fax: (303) 792-5333
*http://www.amerhumane.org*

Provides national leadership in the development of programs, policies, and services on behalf of abused and neglected children through training, consultation, research, advocacy, and information dissemination.

### American Professional Society on the Abuse of Children

The University of Chicago
School of Social Service Administration
332 South Michigan Avenue, #1600
Chicago, IL 60604
312/554-0166
*http://www.apsac.org*

APSAC is a multidisciplinary society for professionals who work daily with the problems caused by child abuse. APSAC's goals are to facilitate communication between disciplines; to promote interdisciplinary standards for identification, assessment, and treatment; and to enhance the well-being of professionals in this difficult field.

### Child Welfare League of America

440 First Street NW, 3rd Floor
Washington, DC 20001
202/638-2952
*http://www.cwla.org*

The CWLA is a federation of nearly 1,000 member agencies in the United States and Canada, both public and voluntary, who employ more than 150,000 staff and serve more than 2 million children annually. CWLA is dedicated to improving services to abused, neglected, and deprived children and their families. CWLA develops practice standards of service, provides consultation, advocates on Capitol Hill, conducts research and training, and provides the most comprehensive child welfare publications and information service in North America.

### Children's Defense Fund

122 C Street NW
Washington, DC 20001
202/628-8787
*http://www.childrensdefense.org*

A privately supported child advocacy organization, CDF pays particular attention to the needs of poor and minority children and those with disabilities. CDF educates the nation about the needs of children and encourages preventive investment before children get sick or into trouble, drop out of school, or suffer family breakdown.

### Family Resource Coalition of America
20 North Wacker Drive, #1100
Chicago, IL 60606
312/338-1522
*http://www.frca.org*
Works to bring about a completely new societal response to children, youth, and their families: one that strengthens and empowers families and communities so that they can foster the optimal development of children, youth, and adult family members.

### National Center for Missing and Exploited Children
2101 Wilson Boulevard, #550
Arlington, VA 22201
703/235-3900
To report information: 800-843-5678
*http://www.missingkids.com*
A clearinghouse that collects, exchanges, and disseminates information on missing and exploited children.

### National Committee for Prevention of Child Abuse (NCPCA)
332 S. Michigan Avenue
Suite 1600 Chicago, IL 60604
312/663-3520
*http://www.childabuse.org*
A privately funded organization that promotes public awareness of child abuse and community-based programs to prevent child abuse and neglect. NCPCA has state chapters and publishes educational materials that deal with child abuse, child abuse prevention, and parenting. The website lists state contacts.

### National Council on Child Abuse and Family Violence
1155 Connecticut Avenue NW, #400
Washington, DC 20036
202/429-6695
800/222-2000
A nonprofit, private sector initiative to strengthen community prevention and treatment programs through national advocacy, volunteer recruitment and training, professional accreditation and placement, publications, technical assistance, and fund develop-

ment to benefit qualified agencies and organizations in the United States and internationally.

### National Resource Center for Family Centered Practice
School of Social Work
University of Iowa
112 North Hall
Iowa City, IA 52242-1223
319/335-2204
*http://www.uiowa.edu/~nrcfcp/*

Assists governments and agencies in building and improving family-based systems and services through technical assistance, training, research, information, and evaluation.

### Parents Anonymous, Inc.
675 W. Foothill Boulevard, #220
Claremont, CA 91711
909/621-6184
Fax: 909/625-6304
*http://www.parentsanonymous-natl.org*

Parents Anonymous is the nation's leading provider of direct service to families with abuse problems. Parents Anonymous leads a diverse and dynamic national network of more than 2,300 community-based Parents Anonymous groups throughout the United States. These weekly, ongoing Parents Anonymous groups are co-led by parents and professionally trained facilitators and are free of charge to participants. While the parents are meeting, their children are engaged in specialized programs to promote their healthy growth and development. Annually, more than 100,000 parents and their children come together in Parents Anonymous groups to learn new skills, transform their attitudes and behaviors, and create long-term positive changes in their lives.

# Information Sources

### Child Abuse Prevention Network
*http://child.cornell.edu/capn.html*

This website is an initiative of the Family Life Development Center at Cornell University. The network is dedicated to enhancing internet resources for the prevention of child abuse and neglect, and reducing the negative conditions in the family and the community that lead to child maltreatment.

### Clearinghouse on Child Abuse and Neglect Information
330 C Street, SW
Washington, DC 20447
800/ 394-3366
703/ 385-7565
*http://www.calib.com/nccanch/*

This is a federal program that serves as a national resource for information on the prevention, identification, and treatment of child abuse and neglect

### National Directory of Children and Youth Services
P.O. Box 1837
Longmont, CO 80502-1837
800/ 343-6681
303/ 776-5831

A comprehensive directory that lists national and state services.

# Appendix D
## Resources for Statistics


### U.S. Census Data
*http://www.census.gov*

Government census data from the 1990 census.


### National Child Abuse Statistics
*http://www.calib.com.nccanch*

The National Clearinghouse on Child Abuse and Neglect has statistics available from several major national studies. Data are summarized and available in a narrative, easy-to-understand format.


### Federal Government Statistics
*http://www.fedstats.gov*

This site provides easy access to the full range of statistics and information produced by 70 government agencies.


### Child Statistics
*http://www.childstats.gov*

Provides general information on the status of the nation's children.


### National, State, and Local Child Statistics
*http://www.aecf.org/aeckids.htm*

This site, sponsored by the Annie E. Casey Foundation, tracks the well-being of children.

# Appendix E
## Resource Materials

The following publications focus on child abuse and neglect or closely related issues.

## Publications

***Child Protection Report***
951 Pershing Drive
Silver Spring, MD  20910-4464
800-274-6737; in DC metro area: 301/589-5103
*http://www.bpinews.com*
E-mail: *bpinews@bpinews.com/hr/pages/cpr.htm*

This independent biweekly newsletter is an excellent source for up-to-date coverage of national politics, policies, and programs focused on child abuse and many other child welfare issues. The newsletter also provides information about potential national funding sources, new resource materials, and conferences.

***Youth Today***
1200 17th Street NW, 4th Floor
Washington DC  20036-3006
(202) 785-0764
E-mail: *hn2759@handsnet.org*

This monthly newspaper, a publication of the American Youth Work Center, is an independent source of information on the events, issues, and organizations that shape the youth service field.

# Journals

*Child Abuse and Neglect: The International Journal*
Elsevier Science, Inc.
P. O. Box 7247-7682
Philadelphia, PA 19170-7682
212/989-5800

*Child Maltreatment*
A quarterly peer-reviewed interdisciplinary policy and practice oriented journal from American Professional Society on the Abuse of Children (see listing in Appendix C).

*Journal of Child Sexual Abuse*
Harworth Press, Inc.
10 Alice Street
Binghamton, NY 13904
607/722-5857

*Journal of Family Violence*
Plenum Press
233 Spring Street
New York, NY 10013
212/620-8468

*Journal of Interpersonal Violence*
Sage Publications
2455 Teller Road
Thousand Oaks, CA 91320
805/499-0721

# Appendix F
## Sample Child Abuse and Neglect Reporting Policy for Prevention Program Staff

A prevention program's policy for reporting child abuse and neglect should, at a minimum, provide the following:

★ A brief rationale for involving program personnel in reporting

*Because of their sustained contact with families, employees are in an excellent position to identify abused or neglected children and to refer them for treatment and protection.*

★ The name and appropriate section numbers of the state reporting statute

*To comply with the Mandatory Reporting of Child Abuse Act (Section 350-1 through 350-5), Hawaii Revised Statues (1968), as amended (Supp. 1975)...*

★ Who specifically is mandated to report and (if applicable) who may report

*All employees who suspect that a child is being abused or neglected are mandated by law to report...*

★ Reportable conditions as defined by state law

*According to state law abuse is defined as...*

★ The person or agency to receive reports

*...shall report to the Department of Social Services...*

★ **The information required of the reporter**

*...and give the following information: name, address, and age of child; name and address of parent or legal guardian; nature and extent of injuries or description of neglect; any other information that might help establish the cause of the injuries or condition.*

*It is not the responsibility of the staff to prove that the child has been abused or neglected, or to determine whether the child is in need of protection.*

★ Expected professional conduct by employees

*Any personal interview or physical inspection of the child should be conducted in a professional manner...*

★ The exact language of the state law to define "abuse" and "neglect"; if necessary, to explain, clarify, or expand

*"Abuse" means the infliction, by other than accidental means, of physical harm upon the body of a child. "Neglect" means the failure to provide necessary food, care, clothing, shelter or medical attention for a child.*

★ The method by which personnel are to report (if appropriate, list telephone number for reporting) and the time in which to report

*An oral report must be made as soon as possible by telephone or otherwise and may be followed by a written report.*

★ Whether or not there is immunity from civil liability and criminal penalty for those who report or participate in an investigation or judicial proceeding; or whether immunity is for "good faith" reporting

*In New York, anyone making a report in accordance with state law or participating in a resulting judicial proceeding is presumed to be acting in good faith and, in doing so, is immune from any civil or criminal liability that might otherwise be imposed.*

*In Maryland, there is no immunity from civil suits for untrue statements made by one citizen against another.*

★ Penalty for failure to report, if established

*Failure to report may result in a misdemeanor charge: by state law, punishment by a fine of up to $500, imprisonment up to one year or both.*

★ Action taken by Program Administrator for failure to report

*Failure to report may result in disciplinary action against the employee.*

★ Any provisions of the law regarding the confidentiality of records pertaining to reports of suspected abuse or neglect

*All records concerning reports of suspected abuse or neglect are confidential. Anyone who permits, assists, or encourages the release of information from records to a person or agency not legally permitted to have access may be guilty of a misdemeanor.*

★ Any program or agency forms or procedures that the employee must complete

*After making the oral reports, the employee shall complete the Abuse Report Form and submit one copy to his/her supervisor and return a copy for his/her own files.* (See sample form on the following page.)

## *Sample Child Abuse/Neglect Report Documentation Form*

Child's name: _____ Date of birth: _____

Address: _____

**Type of Report:**

❑ Physical abuse ❑ Sexual abuse

❑ Emotional abuse ❑ Neglect

❑ Educational neglect ❑ Medical neglect ❑ Other

**Reason for Report:**

Information reported by

❑ Mother ❑ Father ❑ Brother ❑ Sister

❑ Baby-sitter ❑ Other (describe)

Observation of child/home (describe): _____

_____

Date of report to DCFS: _____ Reported to: _____

**Report Accepted:** ❑ Yes ❑ No

Alleged Perpetrator (name): _____

Address: _____

Perpetrator's relationship to child:

❑ Mother ❑ Father ❑ Brother ❑ Sister
❑ Baby-sitter ❑ Other (describe)

Description of abuse/neglect: _____

_____

**Report completed:** ❑ During assessment ❑ During course of program

_____

Staff person        Date    Supervisor        Date

# About the Authors

**Rebekah L. Dorman**, Ph.D., has been engaged in child abuse prevention for the past 20 years at the national, state, and local levels. She developed Migrant Child Abuse Prevention Plans for the states of New Jersey, Florida, and Maryland; has trained thousands of professionals across the country in prevention; been a presenter at the National Conference on Child Abuse and Neglect; and served as grant reviewer for the National Center on Child Abuse and Neglect. Parenting Plus, a program she directed, was named Outstanding Prevention Program of 1994 by the Ohio Department of Mental Health. Dr. Dorman is a developmental psychologist and vice president of Applewood Centers, Inc., where she heads the Division of Family and Child Development. She also serves as an adjunct faculty member at Cleveland State University. Currently she is engaged in developing home-based prevention programs for parents of young children and for parents of children with chronic medical conditions.

**Douglas J. Moore**, Ph.D., is former director of Research and Training at the Child Guidance Center of Greater Cleveland. Dr. Moore was responsible for overseeing the design of a statewide project that assisted organizations conducting child maltreatment prevention programs. This book is a result of that project. He has extensive experience in the design and implementation of evaluation programs, including those targeted towards child maltreatment. Dr. Moore is currently the managing partner and clinical psychologist for Mosaics Integrated Health in Cleveland, Ohio. Mosaics Integrated Health is an innovative group of professionals integrating psychological, physical, and spiritual services to foster well-being for individuals, families, groups, and corporations.

 **Caroline A. Schaerfl**, M.Ed., L.S.W., advocates actively for prevention education. Ms. Schaerfl has a Master's degree and teaching certification in Specific Learning Disabilities, is a Licensed Social Worker, and currently is pursuing a doctoral degree in Clinical Psychology. Ms. Schaerfl regularly makes presentations to parent and professional groups on child-rearing and educational topics and issues through seminars and radio. Her contributions to the field of child abuse prevention include primary and secondary prevention program development and implementation, as well as numerous psychoeducational curricula aimed at preventing abuse, promoting safety skills, self-esteem, and critical thinking skills. Among these are *Catholic-Oriented Prevention Education, Parenting Exceptional Children, Parents and Head Start: Creative Partners for Migrant Children, Parenting Plus for Parents of Children with Attention Problems and Hyperactivity, Parents and Children Empowered, Let's Prevent Abuse Resource Manual,* and *U.S. Biographies Series.*